*For my four beloved grandchildren,
Greta, Elliot, Wyatt, and Waylon.*

HERE

Poems for the Planet

EDITED BY ELIZABETH J. COLEMAN
FOREWORD BY HIS HOLINESS THE DALAI LAMA

 Copper Canyon Press
Port Townsend, Washington

Copper Canyon Press is in residence at Fort Worden State Park in Port Townsend, Washington, under the auspices of Centrum. Centrum is a gathering place for artists and creative thinkers from around the world, students of all ages and backgrounds, and audiences seeking extraordinary cultural enrichment.

LIBRARY OF CONGRESS CATALOGING-IN-PUBLICATION DATA

Names: Coleman, Elizabeth J., 1947– editor. | Bstan-dzin-rgya-mtsho, Dalai Lama XIV, 1935– writer of foreword.

Title: Here : poems for the planet / edited by Elizabeth J. Coleman; foreword by His Holiness the Dalai Lama.

Description: Port Townsend, Washington : Copper Canyon Press, [2019] Includes bibliographical references and index.

Identifiers: LCCN 2018057044 | ISBN 9781556595417 (paperback : alk. paper)

Subjects: LCSH: Environmentalism—Poetry. | American poetry—21st century.

Classification: LCC PS617 .H475 2019 | DDC 811/.608036—dc23

LC record available at https://lccn.loc.gov/2018057044

9 8 7 6 5 4

Copper Canyon Press
Post Office Box 271
Port Townsend, Washington 98368

www.coppercanyonpress.org

Contents

1: WHERE YOU'D WANT TO COME FROM
Poems for Our Planet

2: THE GENTLE LIGHT THAT VANISHES
Our Endangered World

3: AS IF THEY'D NEVER BEEN
Poems for the Animals

4: THE OCEAN WITHIN THEM
Voices of Young People

5: LIKE YOU ARE NEW TO THE WORLD
From Inspiration to Action

A GUIDE TO ACTIVISM BY THE UNION OF CONCERNED SCIENTISTS

THE DALAI LAMA

FOREWORD

When we see photographs of the earth from space, we see no boundaries between us, just this one blue planet, a natural world that supports us all. Therefore, we have to see humanity as one family and the natural world as our home. It's not necessarily somewhere sacred or holy, but simply where we live—so it's in our interest to look after it.

Today, we are interdependent as never before and yet we still tend to think in terms of 'us' and 'them'. We need instead to consider how our actions, and the way they affect the environment, are likely to affect others. When I lived in Tibet, people were very careful not to harm animals because they were aware that they were sentient beings like us, but we were not so concerned about the environment. We were a small population living in a huge land and by and large we thought nature looked after itself.

We human beings are the only species with the power to destroy the earth, as we know it. Yet if we have the capacity to destroy the earth, so, too, we have the capacity to protect it. Unfortunately, the damage we are doing to the atmosphere happens gradually, so we do not really notice it until it's almost too late. Our dependence on fossil fuels is such that although we were warned long ago about the threat of carbon dioxide in the atmosphere, we have done little to stop it.

Leaders must confront the issue of global warming on an international level for all our benefit. But on a personal and family level too we need to develop a much clearer awareness of our actions and their consequences, such as how we use water or dispose of our garbage, so that taking care of and limiting damage to the natural environment becomes an ordinary part of our daily life. That is the proper way, and it can only be achieved through education.

This book, *HERE: Poems for the Planet,* contains many beautiful, generous poems and ideas for action. It is my heartfelt hope that they will inspire readers who ask themselves, "But what can I do?" to see that there is a way forward—learning to share the earth and its resources, while taking care of it together.

27 June 2018

Tenzin Gyatso
The Fourteenth Dalai Lama

Preface

My personal epiphany about the fragility of our planet — and our responsibility to care for it — arrived over time. A child of the sixties, I became a lawyer to pursue justice for the poor and for those deemed voiceless. As I watched the environmental crisis intensify—and as my children and eventually their children came into the world—my definition of pursuing justice deepened. Addressing human injustice and discrimination, including racism and economic inequality, I came to realize, requires a livable earth.

Thus for two decades I've run a family foundation that works almost exclusively on environmental issues. We have supported causes such as ending mountaintop removal in Appalachia, exposing the dangers of nuclear power, unmasking corporate policies that abet climate change, and litigating on behalf of our planet and its inhabitants.

It can be hard to understand why humans are not doing more to address the accelerating climate change that threatens our existence, why we've let poor and marginalized communities bear the brunt of environmental devastation, and why we've let so many magnificent animals become extinct. After all, virtually every religious tradition views the earth and its creatures as sacred — this is our "common home," as Pope Francis puts it. We're all responsible for stewardship of the earth that protects and gives life to us.

Sometimes I worry it's too late, and I despair about the state of the earth that future generations will inherit: One without moths crowding around lights at the door in summer? One without bees buzzing around flowers, without the four clear seasons we grew up counting on? After I heard a prominent environmentalist speak of the boiling hell our climate is headed toward, I admit that I questioned the point of trying to do anything.

But then I remembered a friend whose son had a brain tumor. She was told he couldn't be saved, and the doctors suggested she go home and "watch the sun set." *No,* she told them. Instead, my friend found the most prominent doctor in the field and set out to have her child treated far away from their home. Thirty years later, that little boy has children of his own.

Just as my friend acknowledged that a hopeful outcome for her son was not assured, it's important for us to recognize that the earth is facing multiple dire threats, with potentially irreversible impact. We have reason for despair, and there are already many losses to mourn. One gift of poetry, as a form of secular prayer, is to celebrate the earth even as we grieve what we've done to our splendid planet and its creatures, the way we might celebrate and mourn a loved one in hospice care.

But even as we grieve, we act. Even if — like Sisyphus — we push the rock uphill over and over again, this effort is better than sitting at the bottom with our heads in our hands. As a poverty lawyer, I always fought for my clients to keep their homes, in the face of the longest odds. Now, as a lawyer and poet, I believe poetry can move us beyond passive mourning into hope and courage.

Percy Bysshe Shelley called poets "the unacknowledged legislators of the world," as they free our imaginations, our profound sense of what's right, our visceral connection to the world around us. "A book," Boris Pasternak said, is a "burning, smoking piece of conscience." In the same way, a poem can spark political action. Or as Audre Lorde put it in "Poetry Is Not a Luxury": "poetry is a vital necessity of our existence. It forms the quality of the light within which we predicate our hopes and dreams toward survival and change, first made into language, then into idea, then into more tangible action."

With *Here*, we want to galvanize readers to address the environmental crisis head on, with enthusiasm and without the paralyzing fear that leads to indifference and inaction. We want to encourage a sense of urgency and hope. Our goal is to reach those already engaged, and those sitting on the sidelines, in a new way.

There are 128 poems in *Here* by a diverse group of contemporary writers from around the world. The poems are organized in five sections:

1. Where You'd Want to Come From: Poems for Our Planet

2. The Gentle Light That Vanishes: Our Endangered World

3. As If They'd Never Been: Poems for the Animals

4. The Ocean within Them: Voices of Young People

5. Like You Are New to the World: From Inspiration to Action

Poets in the first section put us in touch with the beauty of our earth: its mountains, fields, trees, flowers, and seas. They remind us to see, hear, sense, and appreciate anew our "peaceful, living earth," as Valdemar á Løgmansbø writes.

In the second and third sections, poets bring to life the peril that the earth and its creatures face, the "mutilated world" Adam Zagajewski describes. This section asks us to mourn, with Paul Guest, "the polar bear / drifting out of history / on a wedge of melting ice," and to recognize, with Tishani Doshi, "the magnitude of all this." Anne Waldman asks, "Will we fail to save our world?"

The fourth section begins to turn toward the possibility of hope, with poems by children and teens, the young people who are counting on us and on whom we're counting. One of these poets, Lauryn Brown, admonishes us adults that, "Nature has a voice / If only you'd listen."

In this anthology, poets are listening, seeing, feeling, mourning, hoping, and acting. The fifth section's poems are bracing, energizing, and inspiring. These poems ask us to walk our planet as if we "are new to the world," as Wendy Videlock implores. We hope the poems will help us "set the world turning from one moment into / the next in startlement," in the words of Vievee Francis.

We want to leave you, our readers, stirred, surprised, and ready to act, regardless of where you live, regardless of how often you turn to poetry, and regardless of your political affiliation. We want, as Cecil Rajendra imagines, "to crack the carapace of indifference / prise open torpid eyelids / thick-coated with silver" and encourage one another to care for the earth the way we care for our own children, families, and communities. The poets in *Here* come from many nations and cultural backgrounds, yet their poems live side by side in this space, reminding us that we are in this together across geography and identity.

As a final section, we have included an activist's guide written by the Union of Concerned Scientists. The guide details some of the steps you can take by yourself, in community, and in communication with the institutional powers that be. We enumerate actions that require differing levels of engagement. Even a small action taken by each reader who is touched by this volume could influence other people and positively impact our world. We're skipping a stone into the sea, with the hope that it will ripple outward into the future.

In this effort we are far from alone. As scientists continue to study the impacts of climate change, people everywhere are learning what actions will be most effective to prevent its worst effects, from individual and communal to corporate and governmental. People all over the world are mobilizing. Hundreds of thousands in the US attended the 2017 and 2014 People's Climate Marches in Washington, DC, and in New York City, respectively, and millions more marched around the globe. As of this writing, 184 countries have ratified the Paris Agreement on climate. Although the United States government announced its intention to withdraw from the Agreement, many of our cities and states have pledged to carry its commitments forward. People and systems on every continent are addressing climate issues with passion and a sense of urgency.

Most uplifting to me has been the involvement of one of the greatest spiritual leaders of our time, and perhaps of all time, His Holiness the Dalai Lama. Please read and savor, if you haven't, His Holiness's remarkable foreword to this collection.

Editing this anthology has changed me. I no longer feel despair but hope, like a crocus shooting up from the ground, the kind I could count on seeing at the beginning of April when I was a child. As I've read and reread these poems, I've come to believe that together we can solve the daunting environmental challenges we face. Poetry speaks to us and changes us as nothing else can. It's my hope that the voices in this collection — voices of celebration, mourning, and inspiration — leave you as hopeful and ready to act as they have left me.

May these poems help you fall in love again with our fragile and beautiful earth. May we join together to help save her.

Acknowledgments

I will always be grateful to His Holiness the Dalai Lama for his magnificent foreword to *Here*, which illuminates the spiritual crisis that climate change and environmental degradation present for humanity, and to Geshe Lobsang Tenzin Negi, Gary Hauk, and Stephen Sencer, who shepherded this book to His Holiness with generosity and care.

Nor can I thank enough the Union of Concerned Scientists for its work on climate change and for the activist's guide that Pamela Worth has written. Great thanks also to Peter Frumhoff and Suzanne Shaw for their steadfast friendship for this project. All royalties from the sale of *Here* will be donated to the Union of Concerned Scientists.

Three stalwart champions have given generous guidance throughout this process: Liza Bennett, Brett Fletcher Lauer, and David Wolf. Each believed in *Here* from the beginning, and each contributed extraordinary support.

I'll always be grateful to Michael Wiegers and the amazing Copper Canyon staff: Joseph Bednarik, Laura Buccieri, Elaina Ellis, Emily Grise, George Knotek, John Pierce, Sara Ritter, and many others for their bold enthusiasm and for guiding *Here* and me with so much care, thoughtfulness, and tact.

I am thankful to Lee Briccetti and to Poets House for their great collection and for welcoming me to do my work; to Alice Quinn, who used her knowledge and insight to support this project so generously; to Lauren Katzowitz Shenfield and Terry Odendahl, without whom *Here* might well not have happened; and to Natasha Sajé, who provided invaluable advice and support. Great thanks also to William Bennett, Paula Gavin, Marcia Greenberger, and Kristin Houser.

I am so grateful to my family — Bob, Rachel, Matthew, Kim, and Lucy — for their love and support. And to my parents, whose memory inspires me always.

Finally, I wish there were enough space to thank numerous other people who have helped make *Here* possible in countless different ways. There are many other wonderful poems and poets I wish could have been included in this anthology. Thank you to all for your inspiration.

HERE: POEMS FOR THE PLANET

1

WHERE YOU'D WANT TO COME FROM

Poems for Our Planet

CATHERINE PIERCE

Planet

This morning this planet is covered by winds and blue.
This morning this planet glows with dustless perfect light,
enough that I can see one million sharp leaves
from where I stand. I walk on this planet, its hard-packed

dirt and prickling grass, and I don't fall off. I come down
soft if I choose, hard if I choose. I never float away.
Sometimes I want to be weightless on this planet, and so

I wade into a brown river or dive through a wave
and for a while feel nothing under my feet. Sometimes
I want to hear what it was like before the air, and so I duck
under the water and listen to the muted hums. I'm ashamed

to say that most days I forget this planet. That most days
I think about dentist appointments and plagiarists
and the various ways I can try to protect my body from itself.

Last weekend I saw Jupiter through a giant telescope,
its storm stripes, four of its sixty-seven moons, and was filled
with fierce longing, bitter that instead of Ganymede or Europa,
I had only one moon floating in my sky, the moon

called Moon, its face familiar and stale. But this morning
I stepped outside and the wind nearly knocked me down.
This morning I stepped outside and the blue nearly

crushed me. This morning this planet is so loud with itself—
its winds, its insects, its grackles and mourning doves —
that I can hardly hear my own lamentations. This planet.
All its grooved bark, all its sand of quartz and bones

and volcanic glass, all its creeping thistle lacing the yards
with spiny purple. I'm trying to come down soft today.
I'm trying to see this place even as I'm walking through it.

AIMEE NEZHUKUMATATHIL

Invitation

Come in, come in — The water's fine! You can't get lost here — even
if you wanted to hide behind a clutch of spiny oysters. I'll find you.
    If you ever leave me at night, by boat — you'll see
    the arrangement of golden sun stars in a sea of milk

and though it's tempting to visit them — stay. I've been trained
to look up and up all my life, no matter the rumble on earth
    but I've learned it's okay to glance down once in a while
    into the sea. So many lessons bubble up if you just know

where to look. Clouds of plankton hurricaning in open
whale mouths will send you east and chewy urchins will slide
    you west. Squid know how to be rich with ten
    empty arms. There are humans who don't know the feel

of a good bite or embrace at least once a day. Underneath
you, narwhals spin upside down while their singular tooth needles
    you like a compass pointed toward home. Deep where
    imperial volutes and hatchetfish live, colors humans have

not yet named glow in caves made from black coral and clamshell.
A giant squid finally let itself be captured in a photograph
    and the paper nautilus ripple-flashes scarlet and two kinds
    of violet when it silvers you near. Who knows what

will happen next? If you still want to look up, I hope you see
the dark sky as oceanic, boundless, limitless — like all
    the shades of blue revealed in a glacier. Let's listen
    how this planet hums with so much wing, fur, and fin.

PATTIANN ROGERS

A Very Common Field

What is it about this grassy field
that's so familiar to me? Something
within the beings, the form of the place?
It's not within the foxtail, not within
the brome, not within oat grass or red clover
or yellow vetch or the lot of them as one
motion in the wind. It's not the morning
or even of the morning, or of the invisible
crickets, one near, one away, still sounding
in the damp after dawn.

What is it so resonant and recognized here?
A sense like nostalgia, like manner,
like a state felt but not remembered?
It isn't the center of the purple cornflower
or its rayed and fluted edges, not the slow
rise of the land or the few scattered trees
left in the fallow orchard, not the stone path,
not the grains and bristles of stems and seeds,
each oblivious in its own business,
but something impossible without these.

It's more than the increasing depth
of the day and the blue of its height,
more than the half-body of the lizard
turned upside down on the path, torn
and transfigured during the night, more
than the bells beginning their lesson
in the background.

It's not a voice, not a message,
but something like a lingering,

a reluctance to abandon, a biding
so constantly present that I can never
isolate it from the disorderly crows
passing over or from the sun moving
as wind down through the brief fires
of moisture on the blades of timothy
and sage, never separate it from the scent
of fields drying and warm, never
isolate it from my own awareness.
It is something that makes possible,
that occasions without causing, something
I can never extricate to name, never
name to know, never know to imitate.

MARINA BORODITSKAYA

Staying in the Woodman's Cabin

Here the birds fly down
Right into the garden
Here the sky lifts
Straight up from the ground.
If only we lived here
The whole year round —
We'd speak much slower
We'd grow far taller.
Here the hedgehog grunts
And noses in the corner
The old well has a chain
That clinks and clanks…
Look out of the window
The moon is pressing on the pane
Open the door —
The sun is standing on the mat outside.

Translated from Russian by Sasha Dugdale

KWAME DAWES

Shook Foil

I

The whole earth is filled with the love of God.
    In the backwoods, the green light
is startled by blossoming white petals,
    soft pathways for the praying bird
dipping into the nectar, darting in starts
    among the tangle of bush and trees.
My giddy walk through this speckled grotto
    is drunk with the slow mugginess
of a reggae bassline, finding its melody
    in the mellow of the soft earth's breath.
I find the narrow stream like a dog sniffing,
    and dip my sweaty feet in the cool.
While sitting in this womb of space
    the salad romantic in me constructs a poem. This is all I can muster
    before the clatter of schoolchildren
searching for the crooks of guava branches
    startles all with their expletives and howls;
the trailing snot-faced child wailing perpetual —
    with ritual pauses for breath and pity.
In their wake I find the silver innards of discarded
    cigarette boxes, the anemic pale of tossed
condoms, the smashed brown sparkle of Red Stripe
    bottles, a mélange of bones and rotting fruit,
there in the sudden white light of noon.

II

    How quickly the grandeur fades into a poem,
how easily everything of reverie starts to crumble.
    I walk from the stream. Within seconds
sweat soaks my neck and back; stones clog my shoes,

flies prick my flaming face and ears,
bramble draws thin lines of blood on my arms.
    There is a surfeit of love hidden here;
at least this is the way faith asserts itself.
    I emerge from the valley of contradictions,
my heart beating with the effort, and stand looking
    over the banking, far into Kingston Harbor
and the blue into gray of the Caribbean Sea.
    I dream up a conceit for this journey
and with remarkable snugness it fits;
    this reggae sound: the bluesy mellow
of a stroll on soft, fecund earth, battling the crack
    of the cross-stick; the scratch of guitar,
the electronic manipulation of digital sound,
    and the plaintive wail of the grating voice.
With my eyes closed, I am drunk with the mellow,
    swimming, swimming among the green of better days;
and I rise from the pool of sound, slippery with
    the warm cling of music on my skin,
and enter the drier staleness of the road
    that leads to the waiting city of fluorescent lights.

CHRIS ABANI

from **Descent**

2

I have seen many red nights and purple
evenings taut with cold and winterlight,
and afternoons yellow with ripe leaves,
but I have never seen the northern lights
or a comet shower or an alien or a desert crossing
from Mexico, people loping like coyotes
in the floodlight-silver night.
Although there was an evening when rounding a bend
on a river walk in London I saw a heron lift off
and slice the silence with its snakelike head,
all wings and feathers and lapping water.
A crepuscular light, brittle like a saltine, and oh, the salt.

MARK TREDINNICK

Inland

I

West of the divide smells like
Sadness and eternity,
Like ancient history
And forgiveness. Smells like red
Gravel and white spinifex.

II

I take the plane's rear stairs out
Into the aftermath of
Rain down onto slick tarmac.
Canberra. Brindabellas.
A good sheep station ruined.
Not far west, but far enough.

III

West of the divide, the land
Smells like itself, not the sea.
It smells like country, old, old
Rain, like cattle and granite.
Inland the air has the tone
Of sheoak and cockatoo,
Dry creek and geology —
A dry peneplain of doubt.

IV

Wherever you are, the smell
Of rain coming or just gone
Is the smell of the same rain
Locally inflected. Here
It's limestone and politics,
Paddocks and poplars and grief.

V

West of the divide smells of
Lichen and salt and dryness
Itself, bore water and wheat
Silos, crows' cries and distance.
A continent of long time.

VI

West of the divide smells like
Where you'd want to come from if
You knew who you really were.

ESMA'IL KHO'I

Image of Kindness

Learn from this tree:
It offers its bountiful canopy of shade
Over your head
               Rain or shine;
Rain or shine
No matter whence
               You came to it;
And it never,
Not even out of innocent curiosity,
                        Sizes you up:
"Hey stranger! Where are you from?"

Translated from Parsi by Niloufar Talebi

JAMAAL MAY

There Are Birds Here

for Detroit

There are birds here,
so many birds here
is what I was trying to say
when they said those birds were metaphors
for what is trapped
between fences
and buildings. No.

The birds are here
to root around for bread
the girl's hands tear
and toss like confetti. No,

I don't mean the bread is torn like cotton,
I said confetti, and no
not the confetti
a tank can make out of a building.
I mean the confetti
a boy can't stop smiling about,
and no his smile isn't much
like a skeleton at all. And no
their neighborhood is not like
a war zone.

I am trying to say
the neighborhood is as tattered
and feathered as anything else,
as shadow pierced by sun
and light parted
by shadow-dance as anything else,
but they won't stop saying

how lovely the ruins,
how ruined the lovely
children must be
in your birdless city.

SHUNTARŌ TANIKAWA

Landscape with Yellow Birds

there are birds
so there is sky
there is sky
so there are balloons
there are balloons
so children are running
children are running
so there is laughter
there is laughter
so there is sadness
so there is prayer
and ground for kneeling
there is ground
so water is flowing
and there's today and tomorrow
there is a yellow bird
so with all colors forms and movements
there is the world

Translated from Japanese by Harold Wright

JAMES ARTHUR

Wind

it's true sometimes I cannot
stop myself from spilling
the recycling

unpetalling apple blossoms raiding
a picnic
making off with napkins I'm nothing
until I happen
flipping an umbrella outside-in
throwing its owner
into a fumble
pelting the avenue with sleet or dust

at times downtown
riding over galleries of air
so full of high excitement howling
I borrow an old woman's hat
and fling it into the road

arriving with news of the larkspur
and the bumblebee
at times embracing you so lightly
in ways you don't even register
as touch

FRANCISCO ARAGÓN

Far Away

(Rubén Darío)

Ox I saw
as a child, breath
little clouds
of steam, vivid

in the sun, Nicaragua
a fertile ranch
abundant, rhythms
tropic, dove in a forest

of sound — wind,
bird, bull, ax:
the core
of me are these

and these I praise
yes, ox: lumbering
you evoke tender
dawn, the milking hour

when days were white
and rose, and you
cooing mountain
dove, recall

April   May
when spring
was all was
everything

KIRMEN URIBE

Don't Make It a Choice

Don't make me choose
Between the Sea and Dry Land.
I relish living on the edge of the sea cliff,
On this black ribbon the wind waves,
On this long hair fallen from an errant giant.

Of the Sea I love especially its heart,
As idiotic as a great child's.
Now headstrong, wayward, now drawing
Impossible landscapes.
Of Dry Land, however,
I most love those great hands.

Don't make me choose
Between the Sea and Dry Land.
I know my residence is a fine line of thread,
But I'd be lost with only the Sea,
Drown with Dry Land.

Don't make it a choice. I'm going to stay here.
Between the green waves and the blue mountains.

Translated from Basque by Elizabeth Macklin

VALDEMAR Á LØGMANSBØ

Spring Song

Awakening grass under children's feet,
The morning, half-awake, dozes in tranquility,
The sun, slumberingly fringing ravines,
Lays on the beach and the billows a glow.
The bluing sky above,
The summits raise themselves from the flood tide.

The buttercup-covered gullies glitter with dew,
The rivers run soundless into a small bay,
The flowers rise up after the winter's blow,
The grass waves freely where, before, there was snow.
Singing birds in flight,
When a whimbrel chirps, a halibut answers.

Growing spring sounds from foreshore and beach,
Moaning eiders in the dead-calm firth,
Friends and enemies greet each other in the mouth of the river,
And soon they find together in loving couples.
Softly flowing billow,
Peaceful, living Earth.

Translated from Faroese by Agnar Artúvertin

ALFONSO D'AQUINO

Black Bee

Syllables	Silence	Magnetic	Bone
that	mirror	zoom	silence
buzz	silence	of the	
ooze	recess	deep	its
		labyrinth	splendor
inside	radiant	of	erupting
of	in	the	in
my	the	ear	my
head	sand		brain
	filament	returning	
dark	on fire	to	mirror
honey		the	swarm
	solar	first	
lights	and	and	where
are	intrasolar	only	*I saw*
hours	driftlight	hive	all
			the
echo	from the	inmost	night
as	eye	silence	
gold	to the	intense	imaginary
	coming		and
honey	thing	pristine	Africanized
water		golden	
beating	from the	thorn	from
to the	thing	thin-	soft
bottom	to the	ning	dirt
of the	going	out	a
wakened	gold	in	bee
water		the	
		water	

Translated from Spanish by Forrest Gander

LEE SLONIMSKY

Dragonflies in Love

They piggyback in parabolas
of lust, looping through noonbright air,
writing their gene-scripted history
over and over as elegantly
as the hushed wing fluttering
with which an eagle, no more than ten
or twelve yards away, brakes,
before talon-spearing a rainbow trout
that caught fatal sunlight.

Unabashed, as if boasting of
needle quick, nuanced motion,
they knife the air, slice blue light
into shreds of silver
drifting across Oak Pond.
The splash of a frog, slither of a snake
do little to distract from
the aura of dragonflies in love.

A hint of breeze wrinkles the sheen
of silver water, as if suggesting
the great age for which this ritual
aerial merge has gone on.
Bodies of blue, green, black, orange,
wings as gossamer blurry as light,
they dart in diaphanous swerves of longing,
the pulse by which heat shimmers and dances
pounding through their thin bright veins.

LUCHA CORPI

Letter to Arturo

Darling,
the ants have invaded
the bread-box
and parade with a coffin
of bread on their shoulders.

The bluejays are getting drunk
on wild blackberries,
they're all in a row on the fence
celebrating the arrival of summer.

The snails are staying out of the sun
stretching like cats
under the microfronds
of the violets.
(Did you know that snails' houses
have no windows? —
Only a door.)

I sit down in front of an afternoon
that is languidly
counting its minutes
and listen to its emptiness.

You've hardly left
and already I miss the light
caress of your hands
on my hair,
and your laughter and your tears,
and all your questions
about seas,
moons and deserts.

And all my poems
are tying themselves together
in my throat.

Translated from Spanish by Catherine Rodriguez-Nieto

JENNIFER GROTZ

Poppies

There is a sadness everywhere present
but impossible to point to, a sadness that hides in the world
and lingers. You look for it because it is everywhere.
When you give up, it haunts your dreams
with black pepper and blood and when you wake
you don't know where you are.

But then you see the poppies, a disheveled stand of them.
And the sun shining down like God, loving all of us equally,
mountain and valley, plant, animal, human, and therefore
shouldn't we love all things equally back?
And then you see the clouds.

The poppies are wild, they are only beautiful and tall
so long as you do not cut them,
they are like the feral cat who purrs and rubs against your leg
but will scratch you if you touch back.
Love is letting the world be half-tamed.
That's how the rain comes, softly and attentively, then

with unstoppable force. If you
stare upward as it falls, you will see
falling sparks that light nothing only because
the ground interrupts them. You can hear the way they'd burn,
the smoldering sound they make falling into the grass.

That is a sound for the sadness everywhere present.
The closest you have come to seeing it
is at night, with the window open and the lamp on,
when the moths perch on the white walls,
tiny as a fingernail to large as a Gerber daisy
and take turns agitating around the light.

If you grasp one by the wing,
its pill-sized body will convulse
in your closed palm and you can feel the wing beats
like an eyelid's obsessive blinking open to see.
But now it is still light and the blackbirds are singing
their voices the only scissors left in this world.

KENDRA HAMILTON

Southern Living

I am cut and bruised, my nails broken.
I have found love and my lover is ungentle.
There's a many-hued bruise beside my left knee,
three on my right leg at the ankle and the thigh,
a new-formed scar on my left shin where she cut
me — she didn't mean to. But I fear
I grow obsessed, neglect my looks — my hair
grows wild. This is what it is to love in middle life
and I praise God that She has blessed me
with a love like this before I die.

I lavish this passion on my house and garden.
I have never felt this for any man. To walk
through my own picket fence, to climb
my steps, survey what I have done...
the painted ferns and adder's tongue dappling
the shade bed, the azaleas and lilacs
resurrected from the dead, each bed dug
and planted myself, the quartz-hard clods
broken with these two hands, on my knees,
pouring sweat like a baptism —
here I've come to know rapture at last.

The house I had before was small and dark
and I loved a dim, cramped love while I lived there.
The man who shared that space loved nothing
that I loved though in his way he was devoted.
On this barren ground I made my first garden
and watched it fail unsprouted seed by withered stem
by blighted stalk. I fought that soil as I fought
the stony clay of his heart, yet in the end
every precious glimpse of green
went dead brown from the roots.

Let us say the names together:
heart-leaf, barrenwort, rose campion, fairies' thimbles.
Feel the meditative music of the names:
Goat's rue, lady-by-the-gate, queen-of-the-meadow.

To love a garden is to be in love with words:
with potageries and racemes, corymbs, hispids, and corms.
To love a garden is to be in love with possibility
for it can never, almost by definition, ever be complete:
To love a garden is to be in love with contradiction:
ravished by order yet ever open to the wild.
But more than all these, to love a garden is to find
your one true lover, for a garden can't survive its maker,
will die with the one who loved it, with only a sudden
spray of roses in June amid a derelict tangle of wood sorrel
and sumac to tell an eye that can read the land
that either of you was ever there.

MORDECHAI GELDMAN

Almost Flowers

I almost brought flowers you said
and I thanked you
with humility and joy
for almost flowers
would be flowers blossoming in our fancy
in the lusting flowerbed of my soul and yours —
flowers from a field not a shop
budding tiny and quivering in the spring's breeze
white blossoms with dewy leaves
awaking in our hearts a new virginity —
an innocent touch, stunned and drugged
in the miracle of our hunger
also blossoms of angels' trumpets
will soar in the skies of our love
and peach blossoms translucently pink
will drop through the night upon our bed
and with them almond blossoms
vertiginous, joyful, reclusive,
and paper-blossoms where we signed
our names again and again
will adorn our common grave
visible already through the mist of our future
in a plot strewn with violets.

Translated from Hebrew by Tsipi Keller

CHARLES WRIGHT

The Woodpecker Pecks, but the Hole Does Not Appear

It's hard to imagine how unremembered we all become,
How quickly all that we've done
Is unremembered and unforgiven,
                              how quickly
Bog lilies and yellow clover flashlight our footfalls,
How quickly and finally the landscape subsumes us,
And everything that we are becomes what we are not.

This is not new, the orange finch
And the yellow and dun finch
                              picking the dry clay politely,
The grasses asleep in their green slips
Before the noon can roust them,
The sweet oblivion of the everyday
                              like a warm waistcoat
Over the cold and endless body of memory.

Cloud-scarce Montana morning.
July, with its blue cheeks puffed out like a *putto* on an ancient map,
Huffing the wind down from the northwest corner of things,
Tweets on the evergreen stumps,
                              swallows treading the air,
The ravens hawking from tree to tree, *not you, not you,*
Is all that the world allows, and all one could wish for.

JEAN VALENTINE

The valley

The valley
edge by edge
bare field by field
I walked through it through you

rain by rain
cold by cold
root absence
and the purposeful cold

Eye opened
slow
but what is slow

SAPARDI DJOKO DAMONO

Japanese Garden, Honolulu

is this peace? A small glen:
a winding footpath, the sun
resting beneath the flowers,
rippling water postponing
each and every answer

Translated from Indonesian by John H. McGlynn

DAVID HART

Naming the Field

We here call this *grass,* you can pick it
like this, it is the earth's *hair,* feel *hair*
on your head. Pick a *strand*
of *grass,* one of the earth's *hairs,*
you can whistle through it like this,
you can chew it and, spread out,
it is a kind of *carpet.* This is what we call *rock*
sticking through the *carpet,* the rock is not a *strand*
but is *hard,* like my *head,* you see, if I tap it,
but *harder* than *head.* This, flowing through the *field,*
we call *stream. Field* is *carpet* between *hedges*
and *stream* divides it. Is this place the end

of your pilgrimage or are you passing only,
have you become astray here? *Hedge*
is what we call this *flowing* upwards of *shrubs* and *bushes,*
of *runners* and *nests,* of parasitic *blooms.* The *field*
in its *flowing* to us through *time*

is named Saint Alphege's, who was beaten to death
with ox *bones.* These, under the skin, we call *bones,*
you see I am thin, my *bones* stick through almost
like *rocks.* This all around us, invisible
we call *air,* see when I *breathe* my *lungs*
fill with *air.* I have had my place here, I wash my *bones*
under my *skin*
in the *stream,* so as to be *clean*
when the *earth* claims me back. This — *splash, splash —*
we call *marsh.* These *reeds* in the *marsh*
are the long thin gravestones
of those who went straight *down*
thrilling to the call   of the steep deep,

their *bodies* long thin needles — 'This won't hurt,
this won't hurt a bit.' I cannot explain *home,*
it is not *room,* nor is it contained within *stone* walls. The *stream*

is at *home* in *field, rocks* are,
air is, *grass* is, *honeysuckle* is — smell it
and *I* am.

FADHIL ASSULTANI

A Tree

I remember now, in my forties,
a tree
next to my home
beside a brook.

I remember now our secrets:
how she used to spread her shadows under me
bend her branches around me
and slip into my clothes
putting me on
as I put her on
together entering the brook.

I remember now, in my forties,
my stories to the tree about the gardenia
and about the girl
who left us
only shadows over the water.

And I moved away
how far did I move away?
But I still see her
stretch her branches towards me
in order to lift me — to heaven.

Translated from Arabic by Saadi A. Simawe

JOHN CALDERAZZO

Douglas Fir, Falling

Surely,
Somebody must hear one now & then,
A big tree falling on its own.
So why not me,
Hiking in the submarine green
Along Panther Creek among Douglas firs,
Their trunks as wide as my outflung arms,
Swaying wind in the rivering crowns
Almost drowning the steady
Breeze of creek water...

I just hear, behind the tangled wall
Across Panther Creek,
The building fury
Of the tree's descent,
Leaf & branch storms set loose
In the bird-panicked, lichen-torn air.
Swirling trunk dust, slammed
With earth, explodes
From the forest.
The ground quakes, the tree bounces
Once, cracks in three places.

Then everything seems to
Stop — creek water, canopy wind,
Rasping drizzle of needle litter
& shredded bark,
Even my own breath:
All of it on hold
As if to honor the tall life
Of this forest king,
Which has temporarily fallen back
Into the grand jumble of things.

WENDELL BERRY

The Peace of Wild Things

When despair for the world grows in me
and I wake in the night at the least sound
in fear of what my life and my children's lives may be,
I go and lie down where the wood drake
rests in his beauty on the water, and the great heron feeds.
I come into the peace of wild things
who do not tax their lives with forethought
of grief. I come into the presence of still water.
And I feel above me the day-blind stars
waiting with their light. For a time
I rest in the grace of the world, and am free.

2

THE GENTLE LIGHT THAT VANISHES

Our Endangered World

ZEHRA NIGAH

Evening's First Star

When a strong gust of wind,
struck by some thought, passed by,
when the face of the burning sun
was wrapped in an azure scarf,
when the breast of dry land
stirred with the dew of breath,
that evening we were all together.

He who laughed and looked at us,
he was our first friend —
the evening star,
who had, perhaps, for the two of us
appeared a little early.

When that resplendent room
was hazy with cigarette smoke,
when the wormwood of liquor
had sweetened everyone's speech,
every anxiety had its own destination,
every reverie its own course,
that night we were all together.

What a stir there was!
I, engrossed in civilities,
you, delighting in revelry.
The subject on which
we spoke and reflected
was the changing world.
Some talk there was of weather and climate.

When the smoke in the room
got in everybody's eyes,

I opened up the window,
you pulled back the curtain.
He that looked at us with sorrow
was again that first friend of ours —
the evening star,
who, perhaps, for the two of us
that night was up till the crack of dawn.
Evening's first star.

Translated from Urdu by Waqas Khwaja

ADAM ZAGAJEWSKI

Try to Praise the Mutilated World

Try to praise the mutilated world.
Remember June's long days,
and wild strawberries, drops of rosé wine.
The nettles that methodically overgrow
the abandoned homesteads of exiles.
You must praise the mutilated world.
You watched the stylish yachts and ships;
one of them had a long trip ahead of it,
while salty oblivion awaited others.
You've seen the refugees going nowhere,
you've heard the executioners sing joyfully.
You should praise the mutilated world.
Remember the moments when we were together
in a white room and the curtain fluttered.
Return in thought to the concert where music flared.
You gathered acorns in the park in autumn
and leaves eddied over the earth's scars.
Praise the mutilated world
and the gray feather a thrush lost,
and the gentle light that strays and vanishes
and returns.

Translated from Polish by Clare Cavanagh

TIM SEIBLES

First Verse

I admit the world remains almost beautiful.
The dung beetles snap on their iridescent jackets
despite the canine holiness of the Vatican
and, despite the great predatory surge of industry,
two human hands still mate like butterflies
when buttoning a shirt.
                              Some mornings
I take myself away from the television
and go outside where the only news comes
as fresh air folding over the houses.
And I feel glad for an hour in which race
and power and all the momentum of history
add up to nothing.

As if from all the mad grinding
in my brain, a single blue lily had grown —
my skull open like a lake. I can hear
an insect   sawing itself into what must be
a kind of speech.
                         I know there is little
mercy to be found among us, that we have
already agreed to go down fighting, but
I should be more amazed: look
at the blood   and guess who's holding
the knives. Shouldn't we be *more
amazed*? Doesn't the view
just blister your eyes?

To have come this long way, to stand
on two legs, to be   not tarantulas
or chimpanzees   but soldiers of our own
dim-witted enslavement. To utterly miss the door

to the enchanted palace. To see *myself*
coined into a stutter. To allow the money
to brand us   and the believers
to blindfold our lives.
                         In the name
of what? If that old book was true
the first verse would say   *Embrace*

the world.   Be friendly.   The forests
are glad you breathe.

I see now
the Earth itself *does*   have a face.
If it could say *I*   it would
plead with the universe, the way
dinosaurs once growled
at the stars.
                    It's like
the road behind us is stolen
completely   so the future can
never arrive.   So, look at this: look
what we've *done*. With all
we knew.
With all we knew
that we knew.

SHARA MCCALLUM

Why Madwoman Shouldn't Read the News

I know you'll say I'm overreacting,
but my mother's prophesying has come to pass:
Armageddon is upon us. Just look at the evidence:
the carriers of our species at every second
being raped and killed and the rare ones
who survive offing their lovers and children
(or worse, if it can be believed, wearing bangs),
molesters and gun-toters skulking
in every lunchbox, the environment
churning into an apocalypse. Oh, kids,
please save us the heartache and leave
in advance: calmly but quickly
abandon your seesaws and swings. Friends,
do you remember when we were young?
Life plump with promise and dreams?
Me neither. Anyway, who'd be naive enough
now to believe in anything so impossible-
to-attain as happiness or justice? Sure
we had a run of it. Even some laughs.
But the day's arrived, as deep down we knew
it would, and spectacles streaming
from across the globe should convince
even the most skeptical
of our soon-to-be extinction.
Not that we listen to true madmen
anymore, but the older I get
the more certain I become: my father
would have been heralded a prophet
had he lived, would have joined his brethren
and sistren on every street corner, trumpeting
this end from the beginning.

PAUL GUEST

Post-Factual Love Poem

I'm thinking of the boiling sea
and the dream in which
all the fish were singing.
I want to wake up with my heart
not aching like death,
but I am always falling
into terror. I'm a good person.
I grieve to appropriate degrees.
I mourn this season. This moment.
I mourn for the polar bear
drifting out of history
on a wedge of melting ice.
For the doughnut shop
which reached an end
yesterday, after decades and decades.
I'm thinking of the light
at dawn. Of the woman
in Alabama who ordered
six songbirds from a catalog because
she was lonely. Or
heartbroken. I'm thinking
of the four that came
dead in the box, mangled.
Of the two that are
missing. I want to tell you
that they were spotted
in the humid air
winging above a mall.
I want to tell you a story
about the time leaves fell from
the trees all at once. I am
thinking of cataclysm.

More than anything, I want to tell you
this. I want to disappear
in the night. I want
the night to vanish from memory.
I want to tell you
how this happened.

Colombe

C

olumbus from his after-
deck watched stars, absorbed in water,
melt in liquid amber drifting

through my summer air
Now with morning shadows lifting
beaches stretched before him cold & clear

Birds circled flapping flag & mizzen
mast. birds harshly hawking. without fear
Discovery he sailed for. was so near

C

olumbus from his after-
deck watched heights he hoped for
rocks he dreamed. rise solid from my simple water

Parrots screamed. Soon he would touch
our land. his charted mind's desire
The blue sky blessed the morning with its fire

But did his vision
fashion as he watched the shore
the slaughter that his soldiers

furthered here? Pike
point & musket butt
hot splintered courage. bones

cracked with bullet shot
tipped black boot in my belly. the
whips uncurled desire?

C

olumbus from his after-
deck saw bearded fig trees. yellow pouis

blazed like pollen & thin waterfalls suspended in the green
as his eyes climbed towards the highest ridges
where our farms were hidden

Now he was sure
he heard soft voices mocking in the leaves
What did this journey mean. this

new world mean. dis
covery? or a return to terrors
he had sailed from. known before?

I watched him pause

Then he was splashing silence
Crabs snapped their claws
and scattered as he walked towards our shore

NATALIE DIAZ

How the Milky Way Was Made

My river was once unseparated. Was Colorado. Red-
fast flood. Able to take

    anything it could wet — in a wild rush —

    all the way to Mexico.

Now it is shattered by fifteen dams
over one-thousand-four-hundred-and-fifty miles,

pipes and pumps filling
swimming pools and sprinklers

    in Los Angeles and Las Vegas.

To save our fish, we lifted them from our skeletoned riverbeds,
loosed them in our heavens, set them aster —
    'Achii 'ahan, Mojave salmon,

    Colorado pikeminnow —

Up there they glide gilled with stars.
You see them now —

    god-large, gold-green sides,

    moon-white belly to breast —

making their great speeded way across the darkest hours,
rippling the sapphired sky-water into a galaxy road.

The blurred wake they drag as they make their path
through the night sky is called

    'Achii 'ahan nyuunye —

        our words for *Milky Way.*

Coyote too is up there, locked in the moon
after his failed attempt to leap it, fishing net wet

    and empty slung over his back —

        a prisoner blue and dreaming

of unzipping the salmon's silked skins with his teeth.
O, the weakness of any mouth

    as it gives itself away to the universe

        of a sweet-milk body.

Just as my own mouth is dreamed to thirst
the long desire-ways, the hundred-thousand-light-year roads

    of your wrists and thighs.

JANE MEAD

Money

Someone had the idea of getting more water
released beneath the Don Pedro Dam
into the once-green Tuolumne, —

so the minnows could have some wiggle room,
so the salmon could lunge far enough up
to spawn, so that there would be more salmon

in the more water below the dam.
But it wasn't possible — by then the water
didn't belong to the salmon anymore, by then

the water didn't even belong to the river.
The water didn't belong to the water.

SHARON OLDS

Ode to the Last Thirty-Eight Trees in New York City Visible from This Window

A thousand windows look down on them.
One crown looks like a granite mountain
peeling in layers, a thousand breaths
a day. One looks, from above, like a bomb,
an exploded shell, a thousand petals.
One is a thriving colony of green
ants milling, a thousand workers,
one like a swarm of pupae, writhing,
one like chartreuse firecrackers with a
sharp Chinese ideogram
on every fragment, a thousand words,
and one is like a thousand paper cranes,
emerald and yellow. Hundreds of years ago,
here, ash was used to make
a bitter sugar, later to make
baseball bats, and across the Pacific
the U.S. printed human bodies,
as ashes, into sidewalks. Honey locust
thorns were used for pins and spear points,
black locust for fence posts — and snowshoe
hare, and mourning dove, ate
the seeds. Oaks gave acorns, to eat,
and to fatten pigs with — "laws provided
that anyone wantonly injuring or destroying
an oak should be fined according to the size of the
tree and its ability to bear fruits."
Mostly what the trees do, now,
is breathe with us, give us natural
artificial respiration.
All will be cut at the waist, the branches

will go with the usual legs and arms into the wood chipper.
The elm, which once fed partridge and opossum,
is getting out on its own, while it can,
it will not stay to witness the killing,
it died the week the judge ruled.
Several rulers live in sight
of these ancient beings, and one of them,
who sees this grove, every day, has the
power to prevent the pyre, to enforce
his guardianship of this arbor, this land,
and air, and water, and green fire.

DAVID BAKER

Bright Pitch

A few survive, black-
shellacked and
    bannered with ads
    (as, *Chew Mail Pouch*
Tobacco), but the un-
subsidized implode—

faint shadows
of plank rot, straw
    mulch, ghost hardware
    and tractor car-
casses wrecked and ribbed
as things Cretaceous.

Wood barns are,
floating the vast
    fields of Ohio, rarer
    than specks of matter
in the blown heavens.
As: one barn =

10^{-28}
square meters:
    a single nu-
    clear particle in
cross section.
The term being

code at the Manhattan
Project (*couldn't*
    hit the side
    of—) for the rarity

of finding such universe
stuff. The proximate

figure: one gram
per 1,000 earth-
    volumes. But (more
    from our sponsors)
why do we want
to blow to bits

every last speck of things?
—whatever's ex-
    pendable, explodable,
    of no more
good than wood sides
now that sheet-

metal pole barns
have rendered them
    obsolete: fallible.
    So fall they do.
When bomb makers
hit the right

proportions of
uranium to a-
    mass, fabricating
    the first
nuclear blast,
did they know

where such elegant de-
signing would
    lead? As today,
    for instance:
four below, snow
blistering down

Madison Avenue. Here's
a shop window big as (of
   course) a barn door.
      Your Favorite White
Fur Boots! Mittens
in Cashmere!

The door's blocked
open. Hot air blooms
   over the walk, and
      the season's bright pitch:
Come In   Let Us   (toy
poodle, half-nude mannequin)

Blow You Away!

KYLE DARGAN

Daily Conscription

> We can no longer afford that particular romance.
> JAMES BALDWIN

Brother Rickey halts me before I cross East
Capitol. He trumpets that we are at war.

I want to admit that I don't believe in "white"
— in the manner that Baldwin did not — but Brother

Rickey would simply retort that my disbelief
is no immunity from the imaginations of those

who think themselves "white." As we await
the stoplight's shift — so I may walk and he may

holler "Final Call!" between lanes of idle traffic —
I think of race as something akin to climate change,

a force we don't have to believe in for it to kill us.
I once believed in the seasons. (I fantasize

fall as Brother Rickey's favorite — when his suits,
boxy and plaid, would be neither too hot nor

thin.) But we are losing spring and fall — tripping
from blaze to frost and back. And what's to say

we won't soon shed another season, one of these
remaining two, and live on either an Earth

of molten streets or one of frozen light? That's when
worlds end, no — when, after we've eradicated

ourselves, we become faint fossils to be exhumed
by the curiosities of whichever life-forms follow

our reign? I still owe Brother Rickey two dollars
for the paper he last placed in my hand, calling me

"soldier." I don't have to believe that I am enlisted
in order to understand he'll forgive my debt

so long as this idea of "whiteness" sorties above us —
ultraviolet, obliging an aseasonal, unending deployment.

Released by the signal, I advance — my head down,
straining to discern the crossfire from the cover.

BOB HICOK

Hold your breath: a song of climate change

The water's rising
but we're not drowning yet.
When we're drowning
we'll do something.
When we're on our roofs.
When we're deciding between saving
the cute baby or the smart baby.
When there aren't enough helicopters
or news crews to circle
over everyone. When sharks
are in the streets.
When people
with wine cellars
are dying. We'll build dams
and dikes, put stilts
on our V-8s and golf courses,
cut down anyone
who cuts down a tree,
paint our Jesuses
green, we'll grow wings, we'll go
to the moon. Soon.

JOAN NAVIYUK KANE

The Straits

Ledum, Labrador Tea, *saayumik.*
A matted growth beneath the most shallow
depth of snow on record in all our winters.

Pausing upbluff from the edge of ice
I broke from branches leaves to pin
between my teeth and tongue

until warmed enough for their fragrant
oil to cleanse you from me.

Somewhere in a bank of fog
beyond the visible end of open water,
alleged hills were windfeathered —

drainages venous. In routes
along the shore forever slipping
under, I am reminded — in the city

one finds it simple to conceive nothing
but a system, and nothing but a world of men.

FABIO PUSTERLA

Star, Meteor, Some Shooting Thing

That one coming out of a building with a crash helmet
jumping towards an afternoon of tar
and wind against his neck, impatient, savoring
the scent of the two-stroke motor oil
or perhaps of fresh-cut grass, the swift kilometers

that will zip by free of care, pure images
of fleeting faces and bodies, windows
like screens or glimpsed nostalgias, forgettable
sorrows: a light accompanies him. To leave,
just leave, get lost, become
star, meteor, some shooting thing.

Suburbs of nothingness, and in every house
the same blue flame, and clear signs
of frustrated hopes and struggles
that have been utterly crushed.
Dogs on leashes, old folks, playgrounds.
"Do you know that once upon a time some forty head
of cattle used to graze here?" says one,
tapping his foot on the polyurethane surface of the small field.

This is the afternoon: a diffused dazzle,
the unexpected greeting of those you pass by.

Translated from Italian by Chad Davidson and Marella Feltrin

NIKKI GIOVANNI

Walking Down Park

walking down park
amsterdam
or columbus do you ever stop
to think what it looked like
before it was an avenue
did you ever stop to think
what you walked
before you rode
subways to the stock
exchange (we can't be on
the stock exchange
we are the stock
exchanged)

did you ever maybe wonder
what grass was like before
they rolled it
into a ball and called
it central park
where syphilitic dogs
and their two-legged tubercular
masters fertilize
the corners and side-walks
ever want to know what would happen
if your life could be fertilized
by a love thought
from a loved one
who loves you

ever look south
on a clear day and not see
time's squares but see

tall Birch trees with sycamores
touching hands
and see gazelles running playfully
after the lions
ever hear the antelope bark
from the third floor apartment

ever, did you ever, sit down
and wonder about what freedom's freedom
would bring
it's so easy to be free
you start by loving yourself
then those who look like you
all else will come
naturally

ever wonder why
so much asphalt was laid
in so little space
probably so we would forget
the Iroquois, Algonquin
and Mohicans who could caress
the earth

ever think what Harlem would be
like if our herbs and roots and elephant ears
grew sending
a cacophony of sound to us
the parrot parroting black is beautiful black is beautiful
owls sending out whooooo's making love…
and me and you just sitting in the sun trying
to find a way to get a banana tree from one of the monkeys
koala bears in the trees laughing at our listlessness

ever think it's possible
for us to be
happy

SHARIF S. ELMUSA

Snapshots

In the blink of an eye
flesh and cement
take over its ancient hills.

No river wets its throat.
The wisps of grass
turn yellow
under the first footfalls
of summer,

and the few birds
that come by
look puzzled, pained
like migrant workers.

▼

Up and down the steep hills,
cars, humped like camels,
issue their pleas.

In the minaret
God gets used
to loudspeakers.

HUANG CANRAN

Come Back to the Mountain

As sunlight is gliding over from the nearby summit,
he stands halfway up the mountain, on a stone
topped with young grass, gazing down
at the swarm of the city's buildings veiled in smog,
and says with a smile that from this slope where
the air is fresh, the sight below makes
one feel like an aged man growing wise and tolerant
— he's such a man —
who recalls the chaos of his early years;
that he too is calm now, the daily company of trees,
flowers and birds puts him at ease,
especially, if gloomy, he will remember that
early next morning he'll be here again,
how suddenly he feels a peculiar joy
— the same joy on his face:
his two rows of neat teeth and ruddy skin
remind me of the sunlight about to arrive,
and if I am on a street under smog,
or in front of a fruit stand, or in a cafe,
I cannot but think of good.

Translated from Chinese by Ha Jin

PABLO MEDINA

The Floating Island

...brillando contra el sol y contra los poetas...
HEBERTO PADILLA

There it is, the long prow
of the Caribbean, charging to break
the map's complexion.
It is a key, a crocodile, a hook,
an uncoiling question,
a stretch of sinews catching
dribbles from the continent
under which it will, forever, float.

The island mouth is smiling
or frowning, who can tell,
stuffed with waning intentions,
sugarcane and sand.

Such a little place, such
an island listing against sorrow
in the middle of the ocean's gut,
playing make believe
queen of brine, dressing up in green
and calling forth its poets for praise,
its leaders for chesty boasts,
inventing for itself a pantheon
of tropical saints, a vast
and profound literature,
an epic history to rival Rome's.

There it is, pretending it shimmers
over the heads of its people,
denying the terror it feels

when no one listens, denying
that it is always almost drowning,
that it cannot help anyone, least
of all itself, that it is only
a strip of dirt between morning and night,
between what will be and what was,
between the birth of hope
and the death of desire.

JOY GOSWAMI

The Burning Bird Drops

Sizzling sound in the water
My sleep broken
A billion years of sleep

Over whose head
The hole of the sky, the iron cloud, and
Under that, circling, the silence of sinking earth

Translated from Bengali by Skye Lavin and Joy Goswami

NATASHA TRETHEWEY

Theories of Time and Space

You can get there from here, though
there's no going home.

Everywhere you go will be somewhere
you've never been. Try this:

head south on Mississippi 49, one-
by-one mile markers ticking off

another minute of your life. Follow this
to its natural conclusion — dead end

at the coast, the pier at Gulfport where
riggings of shrimp boats are loose stitches

in a sky threatening rain. Cross over
the man-made beach, 26 miles of sand

dumped on the mangrove swamp — buried
terrain of the past. Bring only

what you must carry — tome of memory,
its random blank pages. On the dock

where you board the boat for Ship Island,
someone will take your picture:

the photograph — who you were —
will be waiting when you return.

TISHANI DOSHI

Lament — II

By morning she has lost
a husband, a home, a dream,
a night of her life
that will never return.
She tries not to think
of what she will do,
of what this means
in the long history of loss.
There are tigers dying,
she knows, nuclear threats
that might eradicate
the world.
Forests are disappearing,
and seas are being emptied.
She tries not to think
of her hunger
against the magnitude of all this.
Her small hunger against
the failure of civilizations.
She thinks instead
of evening,
how once again
it will grow long and bright,
how eternity that seemed
so paltry just minutes ago
could become eternal once again.
She thinks of the moon
rising in the cleft of the distant hills.
It is the only comfort
she allows herself —
to relinquish the things she loves
as if they were never hers.

MAJID NAFICY

To a Snail

Oh you little home-on-your-back!
Weren't you afraid that my huge foot
Would sweep you away?

Last night, under the rain,
You slid into my sneaker
For shelter.

Today,
You return to your green birthplace
Leaving me covetous, longing for mine.

Translated from Persian by Niloufar Talebi

CRAIG SANTOS PEREZ

from understory

for my pregnant wife, nālani, during her second trimester

nālani and
i walk

to our
small community

garden plot
in mānoa —

the seed
packets in

my pocket
sound like

a baby's
toy rattle —

when do
they spray

glyphosate along
the sidewalks?

from kunia
to waimea,

fifty thousand
acres of

gmo fields —
how will

open air
pesticide drift

affect our
unborn daughter,

whose nerve
endings are

just beginning
to root? —

we plant
seeds in

rows, soil
gathers under

our fingernails —
syngenta, dupont,

dow, pioneer,
basf, monsanto

$240 million
seed sector —

corn for
cattle feed

and syrup —
runoff turns

[our] streams
red — poisons

lo'i — 50,000
heart sea

urchins die off —
what will

our daughter
be able

to plant
in this

paradise of
fugitive dust —

SALGADO MARANHÃO

Of Things

Things, orphans of light,
attack our little tithe

of sky — blue light.
Alive, they writhe

— lava of wandering shades —
buzzing through human glades,

a landscape of our kind,
reflecting the assembly line

of our desires. (Or is it shimmering
forth the very force of glimmering

things themselves?) Junk that seals our eyelids shut
our lives, department stores, that glut

of endless goods. Could there be another way
for those within the web to fray

the plumb-line, plunge a knife
into the fabric of our daily life?

Translated from Portuguese by Alexis Levitin

KIMIKO HAHN

The Fever

for L

The coral reefs are changing color,
the black and crimson bleached away:
the ocean's rising fever,

in every drop the seas over,
damages the membrane of symbiotic algae
and coral reefs change their color.

True, it's less sensational than acts of terror.
True, we can slather sunblock then sunbathe
despite the ocean's rising fever.

After all, the planet isn't boiling over;
algae is not an inflamed country.
It's just coral reefs, changing color.

I wonder if it's, yet again, the ozone layer
ruined by my aunt's persistent use of hairspray —
this ocean's rising fever.

I already own my share of vivid jewelry
from Mother's childhood village on Maui.
Still, the living are losing color
in my ocean's escalating fever.

MAURA DOOLEY

Still Life with Sea Pinks and High Tide

Thrift grows tenacious at the tide's reach.
What is that reach when the water
is rising, rising?

Our melting, shifting, liquid world won't wait
for manifesto or mandate, each
warning a reckoning.

Ice in our gin or vodka chirrups and squeaks
dissolving in the hot, still air
of talking, talking.

W.S. MERWIN

Thanks

Listen
with the night falling we are saying thank you
we are stopping on the bridges to bow from the railings
we are running out of the glass rooms
with our mouths full of food to look at the sky
and say thank you
we are standing by the water thanking it
standing by the windows looking out
in our directions

back from a series of hospitals back from a mugging
after funerals we are saying thank you
after the news of the dead
whether or not we knew them we are saying thank you

over telephones we are saying thank you
in doorways and in the backs of cars and in elevators
remembering wars and the police at the door
and the beatings on stairs we are saying thank you
in the banks we are saying thank you
in the faces of the officials and the rich
and of all who will never change
we go on saying thank you thank you

with the animals dying around us
taking our feelings we are saying thank you
with the forests falling faster than the minutes
of our lives we are saying thank you
with the words going out like cells of a brain
with the cities growing over us
we are saying thank you faster and faster

with nobody listening we are saying thank you
thank you we are saying and waving
dark though it is

Ruin and Beauty

It's so quiet now the children have decided to stop
being born. We raise our cups in an empty room.
In this light, the curtains are transparent as gauze.
Through the open window we hear nothing —
no airplane, lawn mower, no siren
speeding its white pain through the city's traffic.
There is no traffic. What remains is all that remains.

The brick school at the five points crosswalk
is drenched in morning glory.
Its white flowers are trumpets
festooning this coastal town.
Will the eventual forest rise up
and remember our footsteps? Already
seedlings erupt through cement,
crabgrass heaves through cracked marble,
already wolves come down from the hills
to forage among us. We are like them now,
just another species looking to the stars
and howling extinction.

They say the body accepts any kind of sorrow,
that our ancestors lay down on their stomachs
in school hallways, as children they lay down
like matches waiting for a nuclear fire.

It wasn't supposed to end like this:
all ruin and beauty, vines waterfalling down
a century's architecture; it wasn't supposed to end
so quietly, without fanfare or fuss,

a man and woman collecting rain
in old coffee tins. Darling,
the wars have been forgotten.
These days our quarrels are only with ourselves.
Tonight you sit on the edge of the bed loosening your shoes.
The act is soundless, without future
weight. Should we name this failure?
Should we wake to the regret at the end of time
doing what people have always done
and say it was not enough?

LOUISE HERLIN

The gull inch-perfect over water

The gull inch-perfect over water, the busy crane
Call to order a disorganised dawn
    Edged into place by a train

Stone and concrete at the car's pleasure:
The urban monster disgorges louche anarchy
Unchanged by night: rare pedestrians push
    Archaic silhouettes

Building-sites wake, machines shake into life
A dog walks atop a moored barge
    Escorted by a child

And noise gags the day — all-powerful
It makes space a prison
    The trees its henchmen, the season its captive

Translated from French by Martin Sorrell

ANNE WALDMAN

Anthropocene Blues

sound de-territorializes
weather
and my love clings to you
sings to you
in the "new weathers"
within a tragedy
of the Anthropocene

nothing
not
held hostage
by the hand
of Man

can we resist?
will we fail?
to save our world?

we dream replicas of ourselves
fragile, broken
robotic thought-bubbles

inside the shadow
a looming possibility
this new year
to wake up

could it be?

an anthropoid scared
from the forest
slow in development

now infantilized
much like us

stressed yet
perhaps
ready to resist
this scenario?

the forest made the monkey
& the cave & steppe: the human
and now
what makes us suppler
more human?

climate grief?
a fierce tenderness toward
the *destruction* of our world?

questions
or actions?

[*my love for you
sings for you, world
I've got those Anthropocene...
Anthropocene...
blues....*]

LEE HERRICK

A Thousand Saxophones

After Hurricane Katrina — A Poem for the Living and
the Dead

You can live by the water and still die of thirst.
I said you can live by the water and still die of thirst
or the worst nightmare come true:
that body of water taking over the bodies.
Sometime, tonight, see which echoes most —
a whisper or a scream. Make it something beautiful,
like, *We will endure* or *Yes, I love you.* Sometime,
tonight, think of water — how it purifies or terrifies,
cleanses, gives and takes away — think how fast
some things can rise — water, fear, the intensity of a prayer.
Officials in New Orleans said they want to save the living.
I hope they do. But I hope they can also honor the dead.
On Bourbon Street, over 3,000 musicians employed
on any given day. Last night, before I fell asleep,
I imagined what a thousand saxophones
would sound like if they all played together —
one thousand saxophones, different songs,
different tempos, Dixieland, Miles Davis.
Maybe it would sound like birds or bombs,
planes or preachers praising the Word
on a hot Sunday and the congregation saying *Amen,*
some people whispering it, some people screaming it.
Maybe it would sound like lightning tearing
open the sky or a thousand books slammed shut after
a horrible conclusion, or a thousand children crying for their
mothers or fathers. Last night, I thought, how far
would a thousand saxophones echo from New Orleans or Biloxi?
Would we hear them in Fresno? Could we imagine the sound?
Could Baton Rouge? Could Washington, DC?
I don't know what I should tell you.

But I feel like the saints are marching.
They are singing a slow, deep, and beautiful song,
waiting for us to join in.

3

AS IF THEY'D NEVER BEEN

Poems for the Animals

ANNIE BOUTELLE

The Rapture of Bees

Suddenly absent, vamoosed, as if
they'd never been, never spiraled

in air, nor clung to each other
through frozen dark, nor filled

the hive with their million lithe
bodies, packed shelves of wax

and gold, and all that honeyed buzz.
Like a child in a bed in Portugal, just

not there — only space in her stead.
Or hair in coils on the barber's floor,

the neck abandoned and chill. Or
the breast with the other discarded

body parts, somewhere in a hospital
basement and only the stitches to show

where it was. How not to envy
the bees? So fierce an uprush, it

can't be resisted, that soaring in air
to meet whoever is coming, the cell-

phone tower bristling with urgent
messages about the time, the place,

and the fake plastic branches are
arms that sweep them in, not one left,

and death is simple — just being where
the others are, a trembling vibration.

MOON TAE-JUN

The Ibis

Stepping in the mountain shadow on the rice paddy
the old ibis
standing still
A deep thought lingers on the old ibis's body and passes
Like I once stared at an empty pond vacantly
Is this how loneliness lingers?
It was the evening when the mountain shadow fully wetted her ankles

Translated from Korean by Chae-Pyong Song and Darcy Brandel

BETSY SHOLL

To a Bat Fallen in the Street

Crumpled carbon paper, I thought.
Then you moved, humped yourself up
and collapsed, using your wings
like crutches, straining to inch off
the street onto somebody's lawn,
as if you knew the difference.

I bent close enough to see:
your small cat ears, gargoyle shape.
But couldn't bring myself to touch,
to help, as if I were what you were
made to scare off. Terrible,
your struggle to cross. I cringed,
wanting a door to shut, wanting to jog off

like easy belief, thinking the stars
are pure light, not firestorms raging.
But there you were, a glimpse of God
nobody wants — broken body, dark night
with shattered doors, and what sonar
beyond my ears still singing?

MARGARET ATWOOD

Elegy for the Giant Tortoises

Let others pray for the passenger pigeon
the dodo, the whooping crane, the eskimo:
everybody must specialize

I will confine myself to a meditation
upon the giant tortoises
withering finally on a remote island.

I concentrate in subway stations,
in parks, I can't quite see them,
they move to the peripheries of my eyes

but on the last day they will be there;
already the event
like a wave travelling shapes vision:

on the road where I stand they will materialize,
plodding past me in a straggling line
awkward without water

their small heads pondering
from side to side, their useless armour
sadder than tanks and history,

in their closed gaze ocean and sunlight paralysed,
lumbering up the steps, under the archways
toward the square glass altars

where the brittle gods are kept,
the relics of what we have destroyed,
our holy and obsolete symbols.

NICKOLE BROWN

A Prayer to Talk to Animals

Lord, I ain't asking to be the Beastmaster
gym-ripped in a jungle loincloth
or a Doctor Dolittle or even the expensive vet
down the street, that stethoscoped redhead,
her diamond ring big as a Cracker Jack toy.
All I want is for you to help me flip
off this lightbox and its scroll of dread, to rip
a tiny tear between this world and that, a slit
in the veil, Lord, one of those old-fashioned peeping
keyholes through which I can press my dumb
lips and speak. If you will, Lord, make me the teeth
hot in the mouth of a raccoon scraping
the junk I scraped from last night's plates,
make me the blue eye of that young crow cocked to
me — too selfish to even look up from the black
of my damn phone. Oh, forgive me, Lord,
how human I've become, busy clicking
what I like, busy pushing
my cuticles back and back to expose
all ten pale, useless moons. Would you let me
tell your creatures how sorry
I am, let them know exactly
what we've done? Am I not an animal
too? If so, Lord, make me one again.
Give me back my dirty claws and blood-warm
horns, braid back those long-
frayed endings of every nerve tingling
with all I thought I had to do today.
Fork my tongue, Lord. There is a sorrow on the air
I taste but cannot name. I want to open
my mouth and know the exact

flavor of what's to come, I want to open
my mouth and sound a language
that calls all language home.

ANNE MARIE MACARI

Migration South

Early morning along the river, animals pulsing
but motionless —

like the Indigo Bunting resting its small blue body
on a stalk of sorghum,

its head turned west in contemplation. All day
hiking, canoeing, finding

what we could — a Jesus Lizard, crowned, with feet
so fast it could walk on water

if it weren't frozen there trying to look
like a stick, or the Spider Monkey

leaping between trees, arms and legs splayed wide
overhead so it seemed

held still in space. That night, exhausted, I dimmed
the lights, relieved to be alone,

as if I hadn't been able to think all day with
so much life around me, till

in my half-sleep I heard rough wing-beats, not bird

but a harder rasping, and turned to face a cockroach size
of a flattened hen's egg

scurrying behind a cabinet. Up in the thatched roof
I imagined colonies of insects

watching over me, invisible multitude,
and who was I to question them?

Who was I with my binoculars and books?

Not the Hissing Roach or Dusky Antbird, not
a shelled thing with wings

that clicked when it moved, but a frightened
creature of the north,

out of her habitat, no feeble quills on my back,
no gliding from the tree,

just that same falling and falling again, startled

into my bed, into my own featherless skin. Overhead:
clouds of tiny creatures,

the eyes of roaches, moths, broken arm
of the bat, or a bird

trapped in the peaked roof, frantic for release.

RIGOBERTO GONZÁLEZ

The Slaughterhouse

1

Listen.
The slaughterhouse is empty
but you can still hear the squealing —
the echoes, people call them.
These can never leave; they are trapped
inside the walls like stains of blood.

Perhaps,
when the pigs heard their own cries,
they thought they didn't hear their own pain.
All sounds spin inside this house.
They confuse even the pigs.
Pigs don't know when to stop the noise.

2

How strange
that the dogs come near enough
to sniff, but they won't eat the scraps.
They keep their distance, barking,
not at the swine, but at the men
who hang the carcasses on hooks

like coats.
A pyramid of pig heads
stares out the open door: outside
the men wash off their blood-gloves
in a trough bordered black with flies.
The dogs follow to lick their hands

but stop,
taking their liver-tongues back.
The men's hands still stink of knife blades,
of prongs, and of those fingers
that knot the rope so well. So many
smells. But no one smells the same pig.

3
That's me
standing behind a dead sow.
I am tiny as its piglet.
My father took the picture
on my first visit to the house.
I remember it was taller

than church,
but narrow, like an alley.
The intestine strings in the back
didn't look like rosaries then;
they were intestines, running down
to meet the blood pool on the floor.

The sow
looks like she's fencing me off
to the wall, like she has swallowed
half my body. Or is it me
coming out of her pink belly,
born at the moment of her death?

4
Listen.
The slaughterhouse is quiet now.
The gates have lifted to receive
one eyelid for every eye.
Darkness can be so maternal:
blood spots tip down like baby heads.

JANE HIRSHFIELD

The Weighing

The heart's reasons
seen clearly,
even the hardest
will carry
its whip-marks and sadness
and must be forgiven.

As the drought-starved
eland forgives
the drought-starved lion
who finally takes her,
enters willingly then
the life she cannot refuse,
and is lion, is fed,
and does not remember the other.

So few grains of happiness
measured against all the dark
and still the scales balance.

The world asks of us
only the strength we have and we give it.
Then it asks more, and we give it.

CAMILLE T. DUNGY

Characteristics of Life

> A fifth of animals without backbones could be at risk of
> extinction, say scientists.
> BBC NATURE NEWS

Ask me if I speak for the snail and I will tell you
I speak for the snail.
       speak of underneathedness
and the welcome of mosses,
         of life that springs up,
little lives that pull back and wait for a moment.

I speak for the damselfly, water skeet, mollusk,
the caterpillar, the beetle, the spider, the ant.
          I speak
from the time before spinelessness was frowned upon.

Ask me if I speak for the moon jelly. I will tell you
       one thing today and another tomorrow
    and I will be as consistent as anything alive
on this earth.

       I move as the currents move, with the breezes.
What part of your nature drives you? You, in your cubicle
ought to understand me. I filter and filter and filter all day.

Ask me if I speak for the nautilus and I will be silent
as the nautilus shell on a shelf. I can be beautiful
and useless if that's all you know to ask of me.

Ask me what I know of longing and I will speak of distances
    between meadows of night-blooming flowers.
        I will speak
         the impossible hope of the firefly.

You with the candle
burning and only one chair at your table must understand
such wordless desire.

To say it is mindless is missing the point.

GERALD STERN

One Animal's Life

For Rosalind Pace

This is how I saved one animal's life,
I raised the lid of the stove and lifted the hook
that delicately held the cheese — I think it was bacon —
so there could be goodness and justice under there.
It was a thirty-inch range with the pilot lit
in the center of two small crosses. It was a Wincroft
with a huge oven and two flat splash pans above it.
The four burners were close together, it was
a piece of white joy, from 1940 I'd judge
from the two curved handles, yet not as simple as
my old Slattery, not as sleek. I owe
a lot to the woman who gave me this house, she is
a lover of everything big and small, she moans
for certain flowers and insects, I hear her snuffle
all night sometimes, I hear her groan. She gave me
a bed and a kitchen, she gave me music, I couldn't be
disloyal to her, yet I had to lift
the murderous hook. I'll hear her lectures later
on *my* inconsistencies and hypocrisies;
I'll struggle in the meantime, like everyone else, to make
my way between the stove and refrigerator
without sighing or weeping too much. Mice
are small and ferocious. If I killed one it wouldn't be
with poison or traps. I couldn't just use our weapons
without some compensation. I'd have to be present —
if it was a trap — and hear it crash and lift
the steel myself and look at the small flat nose
or the small crushed head, I'd have to hold the pallet
and drop the body into a bag. I ask
forgiveness of butchers and hunters; I'm starting to talk

to vegetarians now, I'm reading books,
I'm washing my icebox down with soda and lye,
I'm buying chicory, I'm storing beans.
I should have started this thirty years ago,
holding my breath, eating ozone, starving,
sitting there humming, feeling pure and indignant
beside the chewed-up bags and the black droppings.

LAURA KASISCHKE

Pregnant at the All-Night Supermarket

Ozone spills over the frozen rolls, the whole

breathing surface of the earth, the whole

unnatural world. Outside, rusty water

yawns up from a well, while
the moon deeply sleeps in her

damp chemise of cheese, while

nurses at the hospital nearby
hover over babies
wearing white. So

much fresh and living flesh
out there — the fish-egg stars, Christ's
mildewed shroud — but here

not even the dim
memory of mold. Here

my hand passes over
what I once wanted to buy — all
those cold loaves and indifferent lies — and I

begin to believe there's nothing left
in this world
I could bear to eat

until, leaving, I see
a luna moth on my windshield.

Its wings are pale green.

LORNA GOODISON

Lepidopterist

> I've done my best to immortalize what I failed to keep.
> JOSEPH BRODSKY

And now I am a lepidopterist
with my rows of bitter pins
securing here, now there
the flown species' wings.
If we soak the memories
in our bile
they will keep and crystallize
come clear
in the heat of this now poisoned air.
I thought I had you / where are you?
You gave up on us / I gave up on you
You changed your mind / I'm changing mine
Lord, even in death the wings beat so.
Hold still
let me put this last row in.

SILKE SCHEUERMANN

To the World's Most Abundant Bird, Once

The last of a kind
what a peculiar task
Given your previous notions
of narrowness and expanse so at odds
with the senior suite at Cincinnati Zoo.
Martha the last migratory dove in the world
what a dilemma you were so delectable
A deli wholesaler
sold eighteen thousand of you in 1855
to hungry New Yorkers
When in your aviary
you miss flying
remember your flock
Thousands of meters wide
or the breeding colonies
fifty times six kilometers How you
when the first European
emigrants came to America
darkened the sky How you kept them
standing for hours in the dark with their astounding calculation
Remembering the time before
their methods of slaughter and railway lines to when
A few wild animals
were a threat to you.

Translated from German by Zaia Alexander

NATASHA SAJÉ

We Saw No Caribou

except on metal signs, the cartooned
antlers ungainly, black against yellow.

Were we not still enough when the heat of day
had dissolved and the animals coolly

made their way into the blue dusk?
We drank their water, ruddled from the rocks,

and shared their air, as clean as absence.
We would have photographed them, of course,

along with the Montmorency Falls, the Île
d'Orléans, notched on memory's belt, accreted.

And if we had beheld caribou, moose — or cougar! —
would the sight have blessed us

like the Shroud of Turin
or simply been allied with one moment,

contained in time by the word *vacation*?
In a Bierstadt painting, they'd be larger

than the Indians, smaller than the sky, part
of the grandeur. Disney would make them

friendly, laughable and safe. In a zoo
we'd say forlorn, circumscribed by fake

rocks and pools. In our photographs
a sheared fur of trees wraps the hills.

Below us the lakes stretch and curl.
Around our bodies an altitude, around

our heads a nimbus. And in the center,
freed of their anchor in God, our eyes

look back at our immanent selves.

TRACY K. SMITH

A Hunger So Honed

Driving home late through town
He woke me for a deer in the road,
The light smudge of it fragile in the distance,

Free in a way that made me ashamed for our flesh —
His hand on my hand, even the weight
Of our voices not speaking.

I watched a long time
And a long time after we were too far to see,
Told myself I still saw it nosing the shrubs,

All phantom and shadow, so silent
It must have seemed I hadn't wakened,
But passed into a deeper, more cogent state —

The mind a dark city, a disappearing,
A handkerchief
Swallowed by a fist.

I thought of the animal's mouth
And the hunger entrusted it. A hunger
So honed the green leaves merely maintain it.

We want so much,
When perhaps we live best
In the spaces between loves,

That unconscious roving,
The heart its own rough animal.
Unfettered.

The second time,
There were two that faced us a moment
The way deer will in their Greek perfection,

As though we were just some offering
The night had delivered.
They disappeared between two houses,

And we drove on, our own limbs
Sloppy after that, our need for one another
Greedy, weak.

MARY OLIVER

The Fish

The first fish
I ever caught
would not lie down
quiet in the pail
but flailed and sucked
at the burning
amazement of the air
and died
in the slow pouring off
of rainbows. Later
I opened his body and separated
the flesh from the bones
and ate him. Now the sea
is in me: I am the fish, the fish
glitters in me; we are
risen, tangled together, certain to fall
back to the sea. Out of pain,
and pain, and more pain
we feed this feverish plot, we are nourished
by the mystery.

The Human Zoo

The peacocks walk along the path between the black trees. They are mystics, dripping with the restraint of beauty. They duck from our gaze, refuse our diamond alleluias, do not encourage touch & we say they are free because they are not in cages. We are happy to repeat this. One male turns his head, the civil crest trembles at our approach. His train of eyes opens like a tree. Unblinking in the face of our overture, he does not admire his emerald-blue life during visiting hours. He does not hide his lack of interest.

DAVID KIRBY

Is Spot in Heaven?

In St. Petersburg, Sasha points and says, "They're restorating
this zoo building because someone is giving the zoo an elephant
  and the building is not enough big, so they are restorating it,"

so I say, "Where's, um, the elephant?" and Sasha says,
"The elephant is waiting somewhere! How should I know!"
  When I was six, my dog was Spot, a brindled terrier

with the heart of a lion, though mortal, in the end, like all
of us, and when he died, I said to Father Crifasi, "Is Spot
  in heaven?" and he laughed and asked me if I were really

that stupid, insinuating that he, a holy father of the church,
had the inside track on heavenly entry, knew where
  the back stairs were, had mastered the secret handshake.

Later we saw a guy with a bear, and I said, "Look, a bear!"
and Sasha said, "Ah, the poor bear! Yes, you can have your
  picture with this one, if you like," but by then I didn't want to.

Who is in heaven? God, of course, Jesus and his mother,
and the more popular saints: Peter, Michael, the various
  Johns, Josephs, and Catherines. But what about the others?

If Barsanuphius, Frideswide, and Jutta of Kulmsee,
why not Spot or the elephant or the bear when it dies?
  Even a pig or a mouse has a sense of itself, said Leonard

Woolf, who applied this idea to politics, saying no single
creature is important on a global scale, though a politics
  that recognizes individual selves is the only one that offers

a hope for the future. Pets are silly, but the only world
worth living in is one that doesn't think so. As to the world
　　beyond this one, as Sam Cooke says, I'm tired of living

but afraid to die because I don't know what's coming next.
I do know that Spot was always glad to see me, turning
　　himself inside out with joy when I came home from school,

whereas Father Crifasi took no delight at the sight of me
or anyone, the little pleasure that sometimes hovered
　　about his lips falling out of his face like the spark from

his cigarette when the door to the classroom opened
and we boys filed in as slowly as we could. Those
　　years are covered as by a mist now, the heads of my parents

and friends breaking through like statues in a square
in a foreign city as the sun comes over my shoulder
　　and the night creeps down cobblestoned streets toward

a future I can't see, though across the river, it's still dark,
but already you can hear the animals stirring:
　　the first birds, then an elephant, a bear, a little dog.

CHIP LIVINGSTON

Punta del Este Pantoum

Accept my need and let me call you brother,
Slate blue oyster, wet sand crustacean,
In your hurrying to burrow, wait. Hover.
Parse opening's disaster to creation's

Slate, to another blue-eyed monstrous sand crustacean,
Water-bearer. Hear the ocean behind me,
Pursued, asking to be opened, asking Creation
To heed the tides that uncover you nightly.

Water-bearer, wear the water beside me,
Hide your burying shadow from the shorebirds,
But heed the tides that uncover you nightly.
Gems in sandcastles, stick-written words,

Hidden from the shadows of shorebirds,
Washed over by water. Waters revelatory
Gems, sand, castles, sticks, words —
Assured of erasure, voluntary erosion.

Watched over with warrior resolution,
Crab armor, claws, and nautilus heart,
Assured of a savior, reconstruct your evolution,
Clamor to hear, water scarab, what the tampered heart hears.

A scarab's armor is light enough to fly.
In your hurry to burrow, wait. Hover.
Hear the clamor of the crustacean's heart.
Heed this call of creation. Call me brother.

KATERINA ILIOPOULOU

The Fox

In the beam of the headlights she appeared
Crossing the road,
A small brown fox.
And again the next night
Flitting behind a bush.
And another time only her tail
Brushed the darkness.
And from then on
Her footprints padded across your sight,
Her warm furry body
Skittering between us.
Always in passing, never staying still.
"But who are you?" we asked her.
"I am," she said, "what's superfluous."

Translated from Greek by A.E. Stallings

SHANG QIN

Rooster

Sunday, I sit on an iron bench with a missing leg in a quiet corner of the park to enjoy the lunch I bought at a fast-food place. As I chew, all of a sudden it occurs to me that I have not heard a rooster crow in a few decades.

With the bones I try to put together a bird that can summon the sun. I can't find the vocal cords, because they no longer need to crow. Their work is incessant eating and they produce themselves.

Under the artificial sunlight
there is neither dream
nor dawn

Translated from Chinese by Michelle Yeh

KRASSIN HIMMIRSKY

The Cricket

In vain we tried to banish him.
The roar of engines did not drive him away,
nor the asphalt with which we covered the fields.
We put up steel fences, walls of cement
                and concrete.
Darkened the air with gas fumes
and shut ourselves in highrise buildings.

But he, like a password,
crossed every barrier unharmed.

And when we claimed victory
in the shade of a leaf, unseen
his fine string music started again.

Its tone reeled off our forgotten friends,
            our forgotten homes,
          our souls.
It recalled to mind
the world's forgotten beauty.

Then we looked for him,
meaning to speak in friendship at last,
but in vain.

He was nowhere visible.
And only within us
still rang and rang his refrain.

Translated from Bulgarian by Denise Levertov

4

THE OCEAN WITHIN THEM

Voices of Young People

The poems in this section were written when the poets were between six and eighteen years old.

NOA GUR-ARIE

Dolbear's Law

To love as a cricket does:
to occupy an ear, a blade
of grass, to see with eyes like
cut stones,
to behold the miraculous
pebbles sitting unprecious,
a hundredfold, a millionfold,
to sing for dirt, to bring cut-up
wings together in hymn and count
time as the sky goes cold, tempo
for temperature, louder even than the
cone-headed katydids, to listen
closely with the crook of a knee for
a harmony of veins, to sing
to be heard by everything, earth and
air and sky and you, muscles
thrumming with the atmosphere,
symphony for the soil.

Buck Lane

winters: mother's voice could   hush like
the smell of pine   and   gasoline.   summers:
shucked ears of soccer balls and
the flex of crickets like boughs of cottonwood
filled the lawn.

afraid, I used to hold fireflies   with
my father's work gloves.
clutching them   too
tight, I   hadn't yet learned
to be gentle with God.

once, when my brother heeled down the porch steps
naked
I stripped to my socks   and raced him.
hurtling circles,   we caught the braying of squirrels,
mat-grass
and wind   in our teeth.

Over   the years   we grew tails, our gums
went sweet and darkened   in our mouths.
we were metaphors   for beasts.

JESSICA WALKER

Fox Chase

Last winter, in dim lit candlelight
I would sit out on the iced terrace
cloaked in my gran's old fur coat
silence was soaked up by the late
night traffic on the high street
When the clock struck midnight
the chime could be heard from
Grandfather's ancient clock
it was then that two foxes would
push their whiskered faces through hedges
dancing into the frosted garden
caught between snowflakes
and the waning moonlight
red stained tails tipped with white
my mother would call me in
but I would stay out all night
eyes fixed to the beauty of this
fox chase, he would join me
around one thirty in the morning
my friend, the haunted ghost
with a jagged scar up his wrist
he would sing to me, and it was bliss

CATRIONA BOLT

The Eloquent Crane

I

Crystalline air and shadows
surround the haiku of my
wingbeat
heartbeat
songbeak
opening to call a harshening cry
on the echoing air.

II

Mountain air falling
As a river through feathers
And haunted sunlight.

III

Catch my form
in its unrivalled gauche detailing—
splaying wings and
endless daddy longlegs' legs.

IV

The descent is flustered,
the picture of ruffled feathers.

V

Stillness on one leg
Caught as a clear-cut tableau:
The Eloquent Crane.

KIRA PELOWITZ

In the Summer

in the summer, I write ripe poems;
I write honey and sun poems;
I write fermenting poems, I write mushroom poems;
I write sweet-scent dirt poems.

nothing is ripe here during the summer,
but I don't write char poems;
I don't write dust poems;
I don't write poems slick with sweat.

I write wind and sandstone poems instead;
I write poems where the wind makes the mountains a flute;
I write ribcage and hipbone poems;
I write poems that crumple below the weight of swollen
stone-fruits.

I don't write poems that wake up damp;
I don't write parched poems, or
poems that shrivel around the edges;
I don't write sunburnt poems.

I write heartbeat and blood poems that disguise as love poems instead;
I write rain poems disguised as love poems, and
love poems that pool on the collarbones of rain poems, and
I write lying poems instead.

I don't write moist-palmed nervous poems, or
poems that have to catch their breath,
but I do write moon poems, and
oyster poems instead.

I write sulfur-geyser poems.
I write deep-sea, translucent poems.
I write night-time poems, and I
write moon poems instead.

because I cannot reach the moon:
I write lying poems filled with rain;
I write poems full of the sumptuous night
and poems that ripple when touched.

I write moon poems that hide in oyster poems,
and palm poems full of oysters;
I write poems where I drink the moon
slick, and soft, and cool.

MARY ANNE CLARK

The Arctic Tern's Prayer

Tell the air to hold me in the rushing heart of it
And keep its paths straight
Away from home let there be a land that
Flows with fish and flies
And let it taste like it tasted at home
Home take this salty scent of home from my head
Cut away the memory of its last ultraviolet
Flash beautiful beneath me
Don't turn me to a twist of salt to fall to
Sea's saltiness if I look back at my home
Let me look back just once let me
Look back

GRIFFON BANNON

How to Be a Hawk

Feel the wind on your face.
Soar across the sky
with your huge wing span,
five feet of bronze wings flapping.
Focus on the mouse running away.
Scoop him up.
Think: "My chicks are hungry."

Screech as you spy other animals,
and watch them retreat
to holes, nests, and crevices.

Enjoy being the predator.
Sink your shimmering gray talons
into the wing
of an old vulture, a common fight
for your territory.
Bring him down.

Soar across the land feeling
proud of your hawk's sight.

Rule the air.

CORINNA DAVIDSON

Rules of the Mouse

Scurry, nibble, nose twitch, hide.
Those are the instructions I hear inside.

No others know the steady beat
I follow as I move my feet.

Ear perk, climb up, higher than high;
Feels like I could touch the sky.

Smaller than small, faster than lightning,
Still there are those who find me frightening.

Heart pound, dodge paw, stay alive;
Here is my pressure to survive.

Those who die, they are the fools.
Those who live have these same rules:

Scurry, nibble, nose twitch, hide.
By these rules I must abide.

BETYE ARRASTIA-NOWAK

I Am Like a Caterpillar

Scared like a caterpillar
Slow, young, and unlearned.
Waiting, waiting,
Until I can change
Into something great,
Wise and brave.
For a long time I watch, listen, and learn.
For a long time I tried to live the life I was given,
But something comes to take it away.
Have I not been patient?
Have I not been patient?

On summer's wake,
I changed into something grand.

MAYA ROE

Midmorning, Summer Rain

I awoke to the rain
whispering down among the birches.
The fields were calling me.

Queen Anne's Lace. Black-Eyed Susan
bowed with dewdrops.
Late raspberries
like blessing.
Everything clean and misty is a gift.

Walking down the muddy road,
barefoot in the morning.

Friends from dreams who follow me
along the central margin of wet grass,
tell me of the things I love,
but do not yet understand.

TALIN TAHAJIAN

Variations on a Mountain Skink

I

I want to know
the smallest things, quiet
    contained. This is where
we crossed the river:
        too far
to swim back. Think of minnows
    when you go, swimming miles,
used for bait.

II

There were too many lizards
on the patio. 99 ways
    to think about skin.
In August, we count 5 species:
    red-backed whiptail,
        desert night,
    mountain skink,
spiny-tailed iguana, Arizona
chameleon. We identify
    with the skink: thin, smooth,
        carnivorous.

III

Yesterday, I watched a skink die:
    leaping from the pavement
& shivering. Rolling to its back, exposing
silver underbelly. Eyes like black mints,
unwavering. Its tail was the first
to go. Some lizards shed
    their tails — this one

abandoned it. I buried it next to the river
in one of your white-stained socks.
I like to think of water.

    IV

We liked to sleep on the patio. I keep
a pair of your socks in the dresser, top
drawer. After scars roll over
    & blisters heal, after the tide of skin
moves through a full cycle, your memory
doesn't ebb. It's always there,
    like blood beneath flesh
or the Milky Way during daylight,
        Hidden.

JULIA BECKWITH

every sunrise is a sunset, somewhere

after *Sand Dunes, Sunrise, Death Valley National Monument,
California* by Ansel Adams, 1948

did you know, light doesn't always come from the sun. sometimes, rays
      shine from the antisolar
point (the sky-space opposite the sun). the negative place has a name, the
      absence of a
distinguishing feature its hallmark
did you know, if concentrated light is shot into a stream of water, it will
      not continue forward.
it will follow the path of the water:
bent,
falling,
the Molten, holding the Intangible
(even something that travels at twohundredninetyninemillion,
      sevenhundredninetytwothousand,
fourhundredfiftyeight meters per second can be
captured / trapped / held)
did you know, it is likely that black holes contain a lot of light — it just
      can't escape
maybe, black holes are the brightest places in the universe
(what is dark matter
but a place that requires patience?)
light makes sense in the abstract but
still — i do not know the sunrise.

RYAN P. COREY

Sparkle Rock

the spikes sparkle in the way of the sun

the spikes sparkle on the logs

the logs are in the way of the water

the water is calm

the rocks might wobble

ducks come in and quack

let's all shout — water

OLIVIA KEENER

The Peaceful Lake

based on a painting by Thomas Cole

In my boat
on the lake
the sun is setting
in the scarlet sky.

The lake is peaceful in the evening.

I paddle once,
swoosh,
swish,
quiet.
My mind goes blank.

ELA ASTER

On the Street of Nature

On the street of nature
the flowers all bloom
and make the world alive.

On the street of nature
the stream sings its song
and bubbles the world around.

On the street of nature
the trees all sway
and dance along with the wind.

On the street of nature
the animals play and jump
all around the world.

On the street of nature
the sky is blue
and white swirls around with it.

HADLEY

The Mighty Guardian

The mighty oak tree stands
straight and tall in his forest home.

His leafy arms outstretch
to soak the sun's warmth and energy.

He thirstily drinks
the nourishment of rainwater punch.

Like a loving father, he cradles the small creatures
that have come for a short visit.

He listens to the forest symphony, the whispers from the wind,
and the sounds of danger.

The storms rush in. The two-legged hunters invade the forest.
The guardian oak moans his warning and bends to protect his
        forest animals.

The mighty oak watches with pride and amazement as the seasons come
        and go —
the cycle of life renews the forest.

Through it all, the venerable oak stands
as sentinel and mighty guardian of his forest home.

MICHAELA COPLEN

Appalachian *Altibajos*

If you asked me for a translation,
    I would point to the horizon as it dips and swells
    in its effort to steady the sky.

I would pronounce it in the rustling of the mountains,
    heads bowed for all that dies in us,
        as they bury their weariness
        in the comfort of the valley's waiting arms.

I would spell it in the upward winding of trails
    that lace themselves into the ground
        and the tautness of trees
        swaying between stability and circumstance.

I would call it "noun":
    as in the way the wind opens your chest and crucifies you
        even as the earth pulls your heart
        down to her stomach.

When you asked me for it in a sentence,
    I would show you where I stood —
    afraid that I would fall and afraid that I would jump and afraid that I
        wouldn't —
    and tell you how
    I felt the words climbing the steepness of my rocky soul,
        but feared the reverberating reality of sound.

And when at last you turned away,

    I would whisper to the hills

te amo   *te amo*   *te amo.*

ALEJANDRO ESPARZA

On the Street of Sky

On the street of sky
the birds are selling hot dogs.

On the street of sky
paint is made out of lightning bolts.

On the street of sky
airplanes are houses.

On the street of sky
cars are made of clouds.

On the street of sky
eagles rule the world.

On the street of sky
water is made out of spirits.

SELENE JAZMÍN VENEGAS

Quetzalcóatl

Quienes hablan de tí, te recuerdan
Un día en el cual ellos
Están muy felices y
También se sienten como una
Zarzamora fresca, fragrante y jugosa
A la vista de las personas
Las cuales te adoran por eres su dios
Consentido y nunca
Olvidarán tu escencia y
Amor para tu pueblo y
Todas un día estaremos contigo entre
Las rosas más bellas del mundo

Q   Whoever speaks of you, remembers
U   a day when they were very happy
E   feeling like a ripe,
T   fragrant, juicy
Z   strawberry, in the sight
A   of all the people
L   who adore you because you are their
C   favorite god and they will never
O   forget your essence and
A   love for your town and
T   we will be with you every day among
L   the most beautiful roses in the world.

LAURYN BROWN

Voice

I can hear it,
the whispers of the trees,
melody of the wind,
the woven tale of the soil,
echoing into the past,
into the future.
Nature has a voice
If only you'd listen.

MAIA ROSENFELD

Snapchat Summer

I press my thumb to the screen,
hold down the half-eaten pie next to your name
and watch as you giggle-shriek
with shirtless boys and almost-shirtless girls clutching red
Solo cups and carelessness.
Your flat-ironed hair falls into the frame, hides faces
you probably won't remember when the time runs out
and these moments are deleted, forgotten
like they never happened.

Your summer hides in an app on your phone, and a million
views won't make it real
enough, your picture frame memories will never be as real
as folk songs and sundresses,
late night whispers about him and then and what-if.
Yours is a pictures-or-it-didn't-happen kind of summer,
an is-that-even-candid type of summer, a temporary, public,
only-'til-you-lift-your-thumb Snapchat summer.

Your summer is pixilated and fleeting.
When your phone runs out of memory,
will you, too?

Sometimes I wonder if sunsets existed before Instagram.
Maybe they just weren't as pretty
without a filter, without followers, without seventy-two likes
to tell them they were beautiful.

KATIE FRIEDMAN

Haiku

Hit rewind and
the flowers will bloom bright again,
rain will revisit the sky

5

LIKE YOU ARE NEW TO THE WORLD

From Inspiration to Action

ROBERT BRINGHURST

The Occupation

for Janet Danielson

I will tell you how it was the world
changed, she said — and darkness
wrapped us round.

I heard her clearly, though I barely
heard the words. It was nearly — yes —
as if she were singing.

Our job, she was saying, is not
to change the world — nor even
to keep it from changing.

No, she was saying (the story
was over already): our only
job is being changed.

How You Might Approach a Foal:

like a lagoon,
like a canoe,
like you

are part earth
and part moon,
like déjà-vu,

like you
had never been
to the outer brink

or the inner Louvre,
like hay,
like air,

like your mother
just this morning
had combed a dream

into your hair,
like you
had never heard

a sermon or
a harsh word,
like a fool,

like a pearl,
like you
are new to the world.

ROBERT HASS

Meditation at Lagunitas

All the new thinking is about loss.
In this it resembles all the old thinking.
The idea, for example, that each particular erases
the luminous clarity of a general idea. That the clown-
faced woodpecker probing the dead sculpted trunk
of that black birch is, by his presence,
some tragic falling off from a first world
of undivided light. Or the other notion that,
because there is in this world no one thing
to which the bramble of *blackberry* corresponds,
a word is elegy to what it signifies.
We talked about it late last night and in the voice
of my friend, there was a thin wire of grief, a tone
almost querulous. After a while I understood that,
talking this way, everything dissolves: *justice,*
pine, hair, woman, you and *I.* There was a woman
I made love to and I remembered how, holding
her small shoulders in my hands sometimes,
I felt a violent wonder at her presence
like a thirst for salt, for my childhood river
with its island willows, silly music from the pleasure boat,
muddy places where we caught the little orange-silver fish
called *pumpkinseed.* It hardly had to do with her.
Longing, we say, because desire is full
of endless distances. I must have been the same to her.
But I remember so much, the way her hands dismantled bread,
the thing her father said that hurt her, what
she dreamed. There are moments when the body is as numinous
as words, days that are the good flesh continuing.
Such tenderness, those afternoons and evenings,
saying *blackberry, blackberry, blackberry.*

MARY RUEFLE

Kiss of the Sun

If, as they say, poetry is a sign of something
among people, then let this be prearranged now,
between us, while we are still peoples: that
at the end of time, which is also the end of poetry
(and wheat and evil and insects and love),
when the entire human race gathers in the flesh,
reconstituted down to the infant's tiniest fold
and littlest nail, I will be standing at the edge
of that fathomless crowd with an orange for you,
reconstituted down to its innermost seed protected
by white thread, in case you are thirsty, which
does not at this time seem like such a wild guess,
and though there will be no poetry between us then,
at the end of time, the geese all gone with the seas,
I hope you will take it, and remember on earth
I did not know how to touch it it was all so raw,
and if by chance there is no edge to the crowd
or anything else so that I am of it,
I will take the orange and toss it as high as I can.

JULIA ALVAREZ

Bilingual Sestina

Some things I have to say aren't getting said
in this snowy, blonde, blue-eyed, gum-chewing English:
dawn's early light sifting through the *persianas* closed
the night before by dark-skinned girls whose words
evoke *cama, aposento, sueños* in *nombres*
from that first word I can't translate from Spanish.

Gladys, Rosario, Altagracia — the sounds of Spanish
wash over me like warm island waters as I say
your soothing names: a child again learning the *nombres*
of things you point to in the world before English
turned *sol, tierra, cielo, luna* to vocabulary words —
sun, earth, sky, moon — language closed

like the touch-sensitive *morivivir*, whose leaves closed
when we kids poked them, astonished. Even Spanish
failed us when we realized how frail a word is
when faced with the thing it names. How saying
its name won't always summon up in Spanish or English
the full blown genii from the bottled *nombre*.

Gladys, I summon you back by saying your *nombre*.
Open up again the house of slatted windows closed
since childhood, where *palabras* left behind for English
stand dusty and awkward in neglected Spanish.
Rosario, muse of *el patio*, sing in me and through me say
that world again, begin first with those first words

you put in my mouth as you pointed to the world —
not Adam, not God, but a country girl numbering
the stars, the blades of grass, warming the sun by saying,
¡Qué calor! as you opened up the morning closed

inside the night until you sang in Spanish,
Éstas son las mañanitas, and listening, in bed, no English

yet in my head to confuse me with translations, no English
doubling the world with synonyms, no dizzying array of words
— the world was simple and intact in Spanish —
luna, sol, casa, luz, flor, as if the *nombres*
were the outer skin of things, as if words were so close
one left a mist of breath on things by saying

their names, an intimacy I now yearn for in English —
words so close to what I meant that I almost hear my Spanish
heart beating, beating inside what I say *en inglés.*

ROSE MCLARNEY

After the Removal of 30 Types of Plants and Animals from the *Junior Dictionary*

Almond no more. *Blackberry* blanked out. *Cheetah* cast off.
But if no *acorn,* because the young will use language for nature less,

by that logic, no *arousal,* brief surge of blood that cannot continue
but lets lives be conceived. If no *bluebell* because flowers are fleeting,

no *beauty* to begin with for these bodies which wither. If no *cygnet,*
the downy being preceding permanent feathers, then no *childhood*

since those who are sheltered under a wing cannot stay, not the same.
As we might wish *mother,* many children's earliest word, will always

be one they hold in mind, can we not let their mouths keep
mistletoe, minnow, and *magpie*? Leave a few things intact,

allow the possibility of turning books' pages in reverse
to *lobster* then *leopard* then *lark,* to the letter of *last* — of *lasting* — of *live.*

ELIZABETH J. COLEMAN

On a Saturday in the Anthropocene,

as I walk in the light of a two-rivered
island to my post office, I mourn

the last typewriter repair shop
in New York going out of business;

mourn that this moves us further
from letters, from connection,

from writing home.
I mourn that it's so warm

monk parrots nest in Sheepshead Bay,
lovely as that sight is, mourn

what we've done to birds:
For 150 million years they saw

their reflections only in the sea.
Then I notice a fire escape

on a two-century-old building
casting a soft shadow; I see wheels

on a bicycle that, like meditation,
seem to slow time. I remember gorillas

stay up all night to groom their dead,
and reading about a woman in Ohio

who gave every building in town
a new coat of paint after she was laid off.

At my post office, endangered too,
I avoid the self-service kiosks, wait in line

for a human. A clerk waves me over
with her smile, asks where I've been.

She tells me about a cruise she's taken
with her mother, describes the buffets,

the turquoise of the ship's pool.
Now I'm smiling too. *What's your name?*

I've been meaning to ask for ages.
Grace, she says, *I thought you knew.*

JAAN KAPLINSKI

From childhood on

From childhood on, I have scribbled on paper —
bowie knives, pistols, men's faces.
Now, one afternoon, I suddenly noticed
I had begun to draw
cats, dogs, horses, and birds.
Although clumsily, with anatomical faults,
but if I continue,
they will perhaps improve,
become more real, more alive,
and, who knows, perhaps even sometime
move, even stretch themselves
or lift their wings
from grayish paper, from between
poems and lecture notes, as once, long ago,
a yellow crane drawn by a student
on a teahouse wall.

Translated from Estonian by Jaan Kaplinski with Sam Hamill and
Riina Tamm

BRENDA HILLMAN

The Seeds Talk Back to Monsanto

& there was heard mourning in the syntax
there was heard brightness in the being of the
land. & there was heard don't.
There was heard nnnnnooooo —
The mountains rise in their noon
of proud fevers. The dedicated grasses wait. In valleys
where basalt meets granite & grains meet valleys
of loam, winds help the free seeds
       of grasses: rabbitfoot & foxtail, they help
quaking grass, the foreign stately ryegrass
Lolium perenne & even the ripgut brome.
Culms of fescue sway as in Psalms. Syllables & glumes. Lemma,
pedicil, twigs & twains, bespuddled musings, ye oddlings, not forced.

      Engineered seeds on faraway farms hear
of the free seed movement. They want no part of Genetic
Use Restriction Technologies turning farmers
    into serfs. *& there was heard mourning in the syntax,*
there was lightness in the senses of the land. The seeds
      talk back to Monsanto. They talk back to AstraZeneca &
      Novartis. They know their root *sed* turned into *sit* & they
refuse to grow. They fold their spikelets inside & sit
    like Thoreau
in a *Don't sprout for Monsanto.* Sit with. the. Don't. d.o.n.t.
don't don't sprout. Sisters, fold awns & bracts to add
power when putting your handwriting on —
      Eco-terrorist seeds won't sprout for Monsanto.
They want no other weather than inside; but they can negotiate
   through poetry, something like::: (1) *would you like to try*
one of our delicious word seeds? or
(2) *stalled were it not for magic, we're trying to decide what to do —*

DAVID HUERTA

Before the Protest in the Street Is Dispersed

The forest of protesters flows like a river

as if it were cautiously advancing
toward the Castle of Count West-West

or Macbeth, Birnam Wood,
the protesters are Macduff,

they are surveyors as well, electricity

travels up and down the column, woods or river
of protesters and that electricity

will later resemble a whip
someone is snapping, but not at the moment —

for now the protesters are pressing forward, filled with lyricism
— filled with literature, they are marching in this poem,

and then the police will come, will cut down
those trees, will dam that river,

will erase this lyricism with the crude prose
of their clubs and this poem will end

as I am ending now
with that final period, barely visible

through the acrid clouds of the tear-gas grenades.

Translated from Spanish by Mark Schafer

FREDY CHICANGANA

Handful of Earth

They gave me a handful of earth for me to live in.
"Take this, earthworm," they told me,
"there you'll plow, there you'll raise your children,
there you'll chew your blessed maize."
Then I took that handful of earth,
I surrounded it with stones so that the water
wouldn't wash it away from me,
I kept it in the bowl of my hand, I warmed it,
I caressed it and began to work it...
Every day I sang to that handful of earth;
then the ant came, the cricket, the bird of night,
the serpent of the outback,
and they wanted to help themselves to that handful of earth.
I removed the fence and gave to each their part.
I remained once more alone
with the bowl of my empty hand;
I then closed my hand, made a fist, and decided to fight
for that which others take from us.

Translated from Quechua and Spanish by Lawrence Schimel

Intersection

The earth shook.   A portal opened.
I walked through it.   The earth shook.
A portal opened.   I walked through
it.   The earth shook.   A portal opened.
I walked through it.   The earth shook.
A portal opened.   I walked through it.
The earth shook.   A portal opened.   I walked
through it.   The earth shook.   A portal
opened.   I walked through it.   The earth
shook.   A portal opened.   I walked through
it.   Ash.   The earth shook.   A portal opened.
I walked through it.   Earth.   The earth shook.
A portal opened.   I walked through it.   Ash.
The earth shook.   A portal opened.   I walked.
The earth shook.   A portal opened.   I walked
through it.   Through it.   I walked.   The earth shook.
A portal opened.   I walk through it.   The earth
shook.   A portal opens.   I walk through it.

CECIL RAJENDRA

My Message

And now you ask
what is my message
i say with Nabokov
i am a poet
not a postman
i have no message.

but i want the cadences
of my verse to crack
the carapace of indifference
prise open torpid eyelids
thick-coated with silver.

i want syllables
that will dance, pirouette
in the fantasies of nymphets
i want vowels that float
into the dreams of old men.

i want my consonants
to project kaleidoscopic visions
on the screens of the blind
& on the eardrums of the deaf
i want pentameters that sing
like ten thousand mandolins.

i want such rhythms
as will shake pine
angsana, oak & meranti
out of their pacific
slumber, uproot them-
selves, hurdle over

buzz-saw & bull-dozer
and rush to crush
with long heavy toes
merchants of defoliants.

i want stanzas
that will put a sten-gun
in the paw of polar-bear and tiger
a harpoon under the fin
of every seal, whale & dolphin
arm them to stem
the massacre of their number.

i want every punctuation —
full-stop, comma & semi-colon
to turn into a grain of barley
millet, maize, wheat or rice
in the mouths of our hungry;
i want each & every metaphor
to metamorphose into a rooftop
over the heads of our homeless.

i want the assonances
of my songs to put smiles
on the faces of the sick
the destitute & the lonely
pump adrenaline into the veins
of every farmer & worker
the battle-scarred & the weary.

and yes, yes, i want my poems
to leap out from the page
rip off the covers of my books
and march forthrightly to
that sea of somnolent humanity
lay bare the verbs, vowels
syllables, consonants… & say

"these are my sores, my wounds:
this is my distended belly:
here i went ragged and hungry:
in that place i bled, was tortured;
and on this electric cross i died.
Brothers, sisters, HERE I AM."

MARÍA ISABEL LARA MILLAPÁN

Kintu

I have gone for a walk in the mountains
And I have asked the wind
If it hides its voice in the trees
I will understand when its roots flower
And dreams no longer wither away,
When our words unite
And evening can no longer distance us.

We will then return with our songs,
When the sun rises
We will allow the forest to germinate
And our spirits to nest in the Earth,
So we can return to live by the rivers
And speak with the birds
Touch the leaves that heal the pain of time
When we want to be ourselves.

Translated from Mapudungun by Juan Garrido Salgado, Steve Brock, and
Sergio Holas

JESÚS J. BARQUET

Robinson

Give me the deserted island, populated
only by scenery and palms.
Give me the sweet and gentle
ferocity of her sea, her sky-colored
breezes, her open seafront, that rambling, run-down house
on the shore. Give me her green
emptiness, her desolate sun, two or three untrod beaches,
even a handful of stampeding angels.
Give me her solitude arriving naked on the limpid current,
so I can once more feel earth beneath my feet,
so I can draw her nourishment again
without saints or heroes or vestiges or notwithstandings.

I promise not to stay either
but instead to let others come behind me
who would then abandon her, too,
just as utopian and satisfied.

JOY HARJO

The Path to the Milky Way Leads Through
Los Angeles

There are strangers above me, below me and all around me and we are all
strange in this place of recent invention.
This city named for angels appears naked and stripped of anything
      resembling
the shaking of turtle shells, the songs of human voices on a summer night
outside Okmulgee.
Yet, it's perpetually summer here, and beautiful. The shimmer of gods
      is easier
to perceive at sunrise or dusk,
when those who remember us here in the illusion of the marketplace
turn toward the changing of the sun and say our names.
We matter to somebody,
We must matter to the strange god who imagines us as we revolve
      together in
the dark sky on the path to the Milky Way.
We can't easily see that starry road from the perspective of the crossing of
boulevards, can't hear it in the whine of civilization or taste the minerals of
planets in hamburgers.
But we can buy a map here of the stars' homes, dial a tone for
      dangerous love,
choose from several brands of water or a hiss of oxygen for
      gentle rejuvenation.
Everyone knows you can't buy love but you can still sell your soul for less
      than a song to a stranger who will sell it to someone else for a profit
until you're owned by a company of strangers
in the city of the strange and getting stranger.
I'd rather understand how to sing from a crow
who was never good at singing or much of anything
but finding gold in the trash of humans.
So what are we doing here I ask the crow parading on the ledge of
      falling that

hangs over this precarious city?

Crow just laughs and says *wait, wait and see* and I am waiting and
      not seeing

anything, not just yet.

But like crow I collect the shine of anything beautiful I can find.

RICHARD JACKSON

from **The Voices**

I. THE GIFT

This plastic cup with the broken handle, green enough to
almost disappear in the grass by the roadside, has come
all the way from its origins in oil, and so it may be the last
gesture of some dinosaur or hold the last breath of an ancient
fern. About the size of a fist, it may have been tossed out
a window, probably from a muscle car, perhaps thrown
in disgust at what was said on the radio news, or held
some bourbon before the driver spotted the police
cruiser behind him. Had he lost his job? Had his wife
left him for his best friend? It hasn't been here long.
The crows are busy with what's been pasted to the road.
Greasy wrappers, newspaper, even a used diaper
tell their own stories. The cup's probably made in China,
probably by some worker not paid enough to buy it.
Certainly the boys on the county clean-up detail would have
bagged it had they passed this way. If I leave it, perhaps
a mouse or an insect will make a home. We all need a home.
Just into the tree line the homeless tent village stays
out of sight. Someone there could use it. Maybe the one
who will thumb his way to Georgia for the onion harvest.
Or I could simply take it home to use as a planter to hold
the miniature, flowerless cactus my wife had left for me.

SHU TING

Maple Leaf

Here is a heart-shaped leaf
Picked up by a gentle hand
On a very special hillside
At the edge of a special wood.
It may not mean very much,
This leaf with its trace of frost

But still the leaf reminds me
Of a twilit avenue,
A mind crowded with thoughts
Released on a gentle breath
That scattered from my shoulders
The rays of the setting sun.

Again, on a special evening
That touch alights on me
Having grown heavy with meaning.
This time I can't deny it,
Deny that intimacy.

Now, when the wind rises
I am prompted to turn my head
And listen to you, leaf,
As you quiver on your twig.

Translated from Chinese by Carolyn Kizer

CHEKWUBE O. DANLADI

My Mother's Sister Schools Me on Her Garden

Pay attention to the moringa saplings behind
those torn bricks; they were birthed on the eve
of bomb blasts, and are therefore always
anxious. See how they weep come any sound?

      Auntie wets her lips, continues.

To be this soil, here, at high noon the
day after a heavy rain, we could never
know the indulgence, the drunk delirium.
What is the word I am even looking for?

      It is something like rapture.

Do you know that we had been growing
potatoes since before the Irish came?
And they wailed from the sweetness of them.
Our earth is kinder, is why.

      A good earth reciprocates generously.

Also, it was these kasa beans that gave me teeth to
speak, to know the difference between
waace and uwaki, so that I would not
curse my mother, as you too should know.

TRACI BRIMHALL

Fledgling

I scare away rabbits stripping the strawberries
in the garden, ripened ovaries reddening
their mouths. You take down the hanging basket
and show it to our son — a nest, secret as a heart,
throbbing between flowers. *Look, but don't touch,*
you instruct our son who has already begun
to reach for the black globes of a new bird's eyes,
wanting to touch the world. To know it.
Disappointed, you say: *Common house finch,*
as if even banal miracles aren't still pink
and blind and heaving with life. When the cat
your ex-wife gave you died, I was grateful.
I'd never seen a man grieve like that
for an animal. I held you like a victory,
embarrassed and relieved that this was how
you loved. To the bone of you. To the meat.
And we want the stricken pleasure of intimacy,
so we risk it. We do. Every day we take down
the basket and prove it to our son. Just look
at its rawness, its tenderness, it's almost flying.

GARY SNYDER

For the Children

The rising hills, the slopes,
of statistics
lie before us.
the steep climb
of everything, going up,
up, as we all
go down.

In the next century
or the one beyond that,
they say,
are valleys, pastures,
we can meet there in peace
if we make it.

To climb these coming crests
one word to you, to
you and your children:

stay together
learn the flowers
go light

GABEBA BADEROON

My Tongue Softens on the Other Name

In my mother's backyard washing snaps
above chillies and wild rosemary.
Kapokbos, cottonwool bush, my tongue softens
on the rosemary's other name.
Brinjal, red peppers and paw-paw grow
in the narrow channel between
the kitchen and the wall that divides
our house from the Severos. At the edge
of the grass by the bedrooms, a witolyf reaches
ecstatically for the power lines.

In a corner in the lee of the house,
nothing grows.
Sound falls here.
Early in the day shadows wash
over old tiles stacked
against the cement wall.
In the cold and silence
my brother is making a garden.

He clears gravel from the soil
and lays it against the back wall.
Bright spokes of pincushion proteas puncture a rockery.
For hours he scrapes into a large stone a hollow to catch
water from a tap that has dripped all my life.
Around it, botterblom slowly reddens the grey sand.
A fence made of reed filters
the wind between the wall and the house.
Ice-daisies dip their tufted heads
toward its shadows.

At night, on an upturned paint tin, he sits
in the presence of growing things.
Light wells over the rim of the stone basin
and collects itself into the moon.
Everything is finding its place.

ROSS GAY

Poem to My Child, If Ever You Shall Be

after Steve Scafidi

The way the universe sat waiting to become,
quietly, in the nether of space and time,

you too remain some cellular snuggle
dangling between my legs, curled in the warm

swim of my mostly quietest self. If you come to be —
and who knows? — I wonder, little bubble

of unbudded capillaries, little one ever aswirl
in my vascular galaxies, what would you think

of this world which turns itself steadily
into an oblivion that hurts, and hurts bad?

Would you curse me my careless caressing you
into this world or would you rise up

and mustering all your strength into that tiny throat
which one day, no doubt, would grow big and strong,

scream and scream and scream until you break the back of one injustice,
or at least get to your knees to kiss back to life

some road kill? I have so many questions for you,
for you are closer to me than anyone

has ever been, tumbling, as you are, this second,
through my heart's every chamber, your teeny mouth

singing along with the half-broke workhorse's steady boom and gasp.
And since we're talking today I should tell you,

though I know you sneak a peek sometimes
through your father's eyes, it's a glorious day,

and there are millions of leaves collecting against the curbs,
and they're the most delicate shade of gold

we've ever seen and must favor the transparent
wings of the angels you're swimming with, little angel.

And as to your mother — well, I don't know —
but my guess is that lilac bursts from her throat

And she is both honeybee and wasp and some kind of moan to boot
and probably she dances in the morning —

but who knows? You'll swim beneath that bridge if it comes.
For now let me tell you about the bush called honeysuckle

that the sad call a weed, and how you could push your little
sun-licked face into the throngs and breathe and breathe.

Sweetness would be your name, and you would wonder why
four of your teeth are so sharp, and the tiny mountain range

of your knuckles so hard. And you would throw back your head
and open your mouth at the cows lowing their human songs

in the field, and the pigs swimming in shit and clover,
and everything on this earth, little dreamer, little dreamer

of the new world, holy, every rain drop and sand grain and blade
of grass worthy of gasp and joy and love, tiny shaman,

tiny blood thrust, tiny trillion cells trilling and trilling,
little dreamer, little hard hat, little heartbeat,

little best of me.

ED ROBERSON

be careful

i must be careful about such things as these.
the thin-grained oak.   the quiet grizzlies scared
into the hills by the constant tracks squeezing
in behind them closer in the snow.   the snared
rigidity of the winter lake.   deer after deer
crossing on the spines of fish who look up and stare
with their eyes pressed to the ice.   in a sleep.   hearing
the thin taps leading away to collapse like the bear
in the high quiet.   i must be careful not to shake
anything in too wild an elation.   not to jar
the fragile mountains against the paper far-
ness.   nor avalanche the fog or the eagle from the air.
of the gentle wilderness i must set the precarious
words.   like rocks.   without one snowcapped mistake

MARK DOTY

Visitation

When I heard he had entered the harbor,
and circled the wharf for days,
I expected the worst: shallow water,

confusion, some accident to bring
the young humpback to grief.
Don't they depend on a compass

lodged in the salt-flooded folds
of the brain, some delicate
musical mechanism to navigate

their true course? How many ways,
in our century's late iron hours,
might we have led him to disaster?

That, in those days, was how
I'd come to see the world:
dark upon dark, any sense

of spirit an embattled flame
sparked against wind-driven rain
till pain snuffed it out. I thought,

This is what experience gives us,
and I moved carefully through my life
while I waited… Enough,

it wasn't that way at all. The whale
— exuberant, proud maybe, playful,
like the early music of Beethoven —

cruised the footings for smelts
clustered near the pylons
in mercury flocks. He

(do I have the gender right?)
would negotiate the rusty hulls
of the Portuguese fishing boats

— *Holy Infant, Little Marie* —
with what could only be read
as pleasure, coming close

then diving, trailing on the surface
big spreading circles
until he'd breach, thrilling us

with the release of pressured breath,
and the bulk of his sleek young head
— a wet black leather sofa

already barnacled with ghostly lice —
and his elegant and unlikely mouth,
and the marvelous afterthought of the flukes,

and the way his broad flippers
resembled a pair of clownish gloves
or puppet hands, looming greenish white

beneath the bay's clouded sheen.
When he had consumed his pleasure
of the swarm, his pleasure, perhaps,

in his own admired performance,
he swam out the harbor mouth,
into the Atlantic. And though grief

has seemed to me itself a dim,
salt suspension in which I've moved,
blind thing, day by day,

through the wreckage, barely aware
of what I stumbled toward, even I
couldn't help but look

at the way this immense figure
graces the dark medium,
and shines so: heaviness

which is no burden to itself.
What did you think, that joy
was some slight thing?

VIEVEE FRANCIS

A Small Poem

for Jen Chang and Martha

From a morning without expectations a surprise,
a word unanticipated and meant. Rare
and jarring. Syllables moving one to tears
when the winter sky is a simple blue, and nothing
is there to impede the dailyness of things. But
the word grows from a note a hello a salutation
and plants itself like a spring dandelion seed that by
afternoon is full grown and blowing more seeds,
lightly, sweetly, a coloratura of delight, and I
feel as if I were both the plucked and the child
plucking the stem and twirling. How a single word
can set the world turning from one moment into
the next in startlement.

A GUIDE TO ACTIVISM BY THE UNION OF CONCERNED SCIENTISTS

In the forefront of our move toward change, there is only our poetry to hint at possibility made real.

AUDRE LORDE

Introduction

Elizabeth J. Coleman

Let's let *Here: Poems for the Planet* — this chorus of diverse voices, urgent and hopeful — galvanize us to address the environmental crisis with fresh eyes and renewed courage. We can have a transformative impact on climate change and environmental degradation through our own actions, and even more so through our influence on others.

This guide to activism focuses specifically on the problem of climate change. However, the ideas on taking action should be helpful in addressing any environmental issue. Although many of the tactics discussed are intended for audiences in the United States, they can be adapted for other countries. And while some content here is time-stamped — technology, modes of communication, and climate change statistics are changing fast — we find it important to start where we are, imagining that these tools will remain useful, with due translation, in the future.

We have put forth a variety of tactical approaches, from those that require minimal effort to those that are more challenging. Engagement with environmental activism is a journey of exploration and of hope for the planet we all share. We might begin our journey with small steps and, as we feel empowered, expand those steps outward. We can use social media to tell our friends and colleagues what we are doing; we can attend marches to gather energy from one another; we can embody the change we want to see. And as we gather confidence for this journey, we can share our accomplishments and joy in this effort and encourage others to come along.

Any action we take to slow environmental degradation is positive; what we want to suggest here is a ladder of engagement. The first rungs we step onto are remarkably meaningful and satisfying, and they lead toward further activities. As we write this in 2018, such steps might include:

- **Individual/household actions.** Shopping with a reusable bag rather than taking a plastic one from the store, just as one example, might save one animal from ingesting a plastic bag or prevent the blight of one plastic bag in a tree.

- **Communicating about our commitment.** As our enthusiasm grows, we might be inspired to share our decisions and actions— no more plastic bags! — on social media. We might join a group of others who care about the environment or start our own group to learn more about problems and solutions.

- **Thinking bigger.** As we learn and become emboldened, we might incorporate other personal decisions; for example, buying an electric car, traveling by mass transit, reducing the meat in our diet, or reexamining our personal investments.

- **Institutional change.** Strengthened in our resolve to have an impact through our actions, we begin to march, advocate, write letters, and show up at legislators' offices or at corporate headquarters.

As people living with and affected by climate change, each of us has a vital role to play. Many sources, including the Union of Concerned Scientists' 2012 book *Cooler Smarter: Practical Steps for Low-Carbon Living*, tell us how we can reduce our own carbon footprint. And though our individual choices matter, climate change is bigger than our own domestic spheres. Once we've examined our own impact, we can and must address the governmental and corporate systems that perpetuate the status quo. Addressing these systems is the branch of activism we focus on in this guide.

We sustain our energy, commitment, and joy as we embark and continue on this journey, giving ourselves credit for what we accomplish rather than demerits for what we don't. As we gain courage, we can take bigger and bolder steps. Since climate change and environmental destruction are caused by people, people can turn them around. We can and we must. My thanks to the Union of Concerned Scientists for this guide.

The Challenge We Face:
Climate Change at a Glance

But we are losing spring and fall — tripping
from blaze to frost and back.

KYLE DARGAN

People worldwide are already experiencing the significant and costly effects of climate change; these consequences will only intensify as globally averaged temperatures continue to rise. In the United States, the most immediate effects, which many of us have already experienced, are:

- **Accelerating sea-level rise.** Global warming is accelerating the rate of sea-level rise and dramatically increasing coastal flooding, especially on the East Coast and in the Gulf of Mexico.
- **Longer and more damaging wildfire seasons.** Wildfires are increasing in intensity, and wildfire season is getting longer in the western United States.
- **More frequent and intense heat waves.** Dangerously hot weather is occurring more frequently than it did sixty years ago.
- **Heavier precipitation and flooding.** More rain falls during the heaviest downpours, increasing the risk of flooding — even far from the coasts.
- **Public health impacts.** Climate change has significant implications for our health, including increased air pollution and a longer and more intense allergy season.

The chart on the next page can help us understand the sources of the challenge we face. As humans, we are overloading our atmosphere with carbon dioxide, which traps heat and steadily drives up the planet's temperature. Where does all this atmospheric carbon come from? The fossil fuels we burn for energy: coal, natural gas, and oil. **To forestall the effects of climate change, we must work together to reduce emissions from burning fossil fuels.**

This chart from the Environmental Protection Agency shows the sources for global warming emissions in 2016. The two largest contributors are

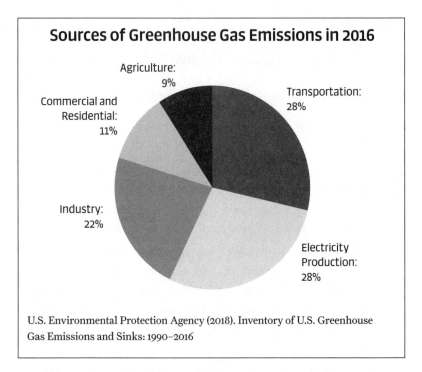

Sources of Greenhouse Gas Emissions in 2016

Agriculture: 9%

Transportation: 28%

Commercial and Residential: 11%

Industry: 22%

Electricity Production: 28%

U.S. Environmental Protection Agency (2018). Inventory of U.S. Greenhouse Gas Emissions and Sinks: 1990–2016

energy use — or how we power our homes and businesses — and transportation. The good news is that we have clean options for these sectors; our job is to advocate for them.

Right now, municipal, regional, state, and federal officials are making high-stakes decisions on your behalf, with your tax dollars, to improve our future — or to damage it. A single state or federal provision, or a corporate decision, can achieve enormous reductions in emissions, far beyond what any of us could hope to accomplish individually. Climate-friendly choices at the institutional level fall into four major categories:

1. Improve energy efficiency in our buildings, appliances, equipment, industries, and vehicles.

2. Ensure that an increasing portion of our electricity comes from clean, renewable sources.

3. Limit emission levels by, for example, setting carbon standards for vehicles, fuels, power plants, refineries, and other major emitters, or by implementing a price on carbon.

4. Invest in research and development to foster new technologies that help reduce emissions.

By getting involved in the development and implementation of government and private policies related to energy use and global warming, you can increase your impact thousands of times over. This guide will give you the tools you need to get started.

Section I:
Reach Out to Your Representatives

will we fail?
To save our world?
ANNE WALDMAN

Anyone making decisions on your behalf needs to hear from you. With a problem of the magnitude of global warming, governments must take a hands-on role in implementing solutions, along with people and businesses. Communicating with your elected representatives is one of the most crucial and effective things you can do to make progress on climate change. We will guide you through:

- Steps to write an effective letter to your policy maker
- How to make a productive phone call to your legislator's office
- How to raise issues at public meetings
- How to set up an in-person meeting with your legislator

HOW TO WRITE AN EFFECTIVE LETTER TO YOUR POLICY MAKER

Letters — even short ones — or e-mails, when appropriate, can have a great impact. They show policy makers that the issue is important enough to you that you took the time to write them personally. Just a few thought-provoking letters over a short period can bring an issue to the attention of your legislator.

Typically, you will receive a standard reply. Since congressional offices process hundreds or even thousands of letters and e-mails each week, staff do not often have time for personal replies. If the reply does not respond to your question or request for the legislator to take a certain position, however, write again and request a clear answer.

With increased security on Capitol Hill, postal mail can take from four to six weeks to reach your legislator. If your message is related to an upcoming vote or is otherwise urgent, send a personalized e-mail (not a form e-mail) or make a phone call instead (skip to the next section for guidance).

Writing an Effective Letter

1. Address your letter correctly. Be sure you have the correct address and salutation. You can find the addresses of all of your legislators at www.usa .gov/elected-officials. If you are sending an e-mail, some offices require you to fill out a web form rather than e-mail directly.

2. Write to the legislators for whom you can vote. Elected officials are most interested in your opinions if you are a constituent.

3. Address only one issue per letter. A letter that addresses one specific topic has more impact and receives a quicker response than one covering multiple issues.

4. Ask for something specific. Ask the legislator to take a particular action, such as cosponsoring a bill or taking a leadership role on an issue. Request that the legislator state a position in a letter of response.

5. Make it personal. Tie the issue to your expertise or experience or to the district or state represented by the legislator. Use your own words.

6. Keep it short. Be sure your letter takes no more than two-thirds of a page.

7. Include your return address on your letter. Your address shows that you are a constituent and allows the legislator to send a response to you.

8. Follow up. A few weeks after you've sent your letter, follow up by writing and sending a short, personalized e-mail, including your letter as an attachment. Offer to answer any questions the legislator may have about your position.

Additional tips

Use your institution's letterhead. If you work in an academic, private, or government setting, consider sending your letter on your institution's letterhead, if this is applicable and allowed. While you should be clear that your opinion is personal, using letterhead may help establish your credibility.

Be courteous. Rudeness will alienate your reader.

When appropriate, express your appreciation. Like anybody, legislators appreciate an occasional "well done." Such thanks show that you are paying attention to your legislator's activities.

HOW TO MAKE A PRODUCTIVE PHONE CALL TO YOUR LEGISLATOR'S OFFICE

Calling your legislator's office is a quick and useful way to communicate your opinions, especially on issues where an action is pending, such as a vote. You will not speak to the legislator directly, but legislative staff track the number of calls they receive on various topics. Just a couple of phone calls over a short period can have a big impact.

Tips for your call

1. Call congressional offices directly or through the switchboard. If you do not have a direct number, you can reach US representatives by calling 202-225-3121, and US senators by calling 202-224-3121. Ask the operator to connect you to the individual's office. If you do not know the names of your members of Congress or want the direct lines to their offices, go to senate .gov and house.gov to look them up.

2. Ask to speak to the aide who handles the issue about which you are calling. Your call will be more influential if you speak to the correct aide. Congressional aides are very busy; if you cannot speak directly with the aide, leave a message with the receptionist stating your views.

3. Let them know that you are a constituent. Elected officials are most interested in your opinions if you are their constituent, so be sure to mention your city and state.

Additional tips and resources

Know your facts. Be sure you have the basic information about your topic in front of you when you call. You should be able to describe the topic specifically and state what you think your legislator should do.

Note your expertise or connection. If you have professional experience with or a personal connection to the issue, be sure to mention it. It will help to establish your credibility and may prompt the aide to ask you for guidance on the issue.

Be brief. Aides receive a high volume of phone calls, so keep your call short.

Be timely. If a vote on your issue is imminent, the aide is much more likely to pay attention to what you say.

Consider calling the local office. If you are calling about a vote or another time-sensitive issue, call your legislator's Washington, DC, office. But if you are calling more generally about an issue that impacts your district or community, calling your legislator's office in your district or state can raise your legislator's awareness.

HOW TO RAISE ISSUES AT PUBLIC MEETINGS

Public meetings are a great opportunity for you to have direct, personal contact with your policy makers and their aides. Legislators regularly make public appearances in their home districts or states, particularly during congressional recesses (generally scheduled around holidays and in summer). Many hold public forums or town hall–style meetings where they accept questions from the public. By asking a question and requiring a response on the spot, you can get your policy maker's position on the public record.

Tips for attending a town hall meeting

1. Find out about upcoming meetings. Call your legislator's local office to find out when and where they will be appearing. Confirm as close to the event as possible, as legislators' schedules change frequently. Some legislators list public meetings on their websites or in newsletters.

2. Prepare in advance. Identify the exact question you want to ask and the key information that you want to raise. Prepare a second question in case someone else in the audience asks your question first.

3. Introduce yourself, state your issue, and make a specific request that requires a specific answer. State your name and where you are from so that your legislator knows you are a constituent. Note any expertise or personal connection to the issue in five words or fewer. Make one or two brief statements about the issue and why it's important to you and your community. Finish by asking the legislator to give their position on the issue or to state whether they will take a particular action.

Get candidates on the record!

Candidates campaign locally in the weeks and months leading up to elections. Attend their campaign events and ask questions to find out where they stand on the issues you care about.

1. **Global warming.** Communities across the country are facing the enormous challenge of protecting people and businesses from the devastating effects of climate change, including drought, out-of-control wildfires, more intense storms, and tidal flooding. And they're trying to do so with insufficient resources.

   Question: How will you support these communities and their efforts to deal with the impacts of climate change? How will you help prevent ongoing and worsening warming?

2. **Renewable energy.** Wind and solar energy deliver reliable and affordable power to millions of homes and businesses across the United States and could be scaled up to provide even more.

   Question: How will you support the accelerated deployment of renewable energy and ensure we modernize our electricity grid to better accommodate a clean-energy transition?

3. **Transportation.** Transportation is one of the largest sources of global-warming emissions in the United States. Vulnerable communities are disproportionately affected by air pollution from vehicles.

   Question: Do you support policies that cut transportation pollution in line with science-based goals? Will you support policies that protect and strengthen fuel efficiency standards?

4. If possible, introduce yourself. Before or after the meeting, make every effort to introduce yourself to your legislator's staff member.

5. Follow up. If you were able to ask your question, send a thank-you note with any helpful follow-up information. If you were unable to ask a question, send a note telling your policy maker you were at the meeting but didn't get a chance to speak. Ask your question and request that the legislator get back to you with an answer.

HOW TO SET UP AN IN-PERSON MEETING WITH YOUR LEGISLATOR

Members of Congress are more likely to support positions their constituents feel strongly about, and there is no better way to display your passion for a legislative issue than by taking the time to have a face-to-face meeting. This is especially important on issues where the opposition is lobbying strongly against legislation you support, as well as on issues that are new, complex, or controversial, where there is an opportunity to educate policy makers. A meeting can be simple and productive. You can meet one-on-one or plan a group meeting with other constituents.

Tips for scheduling a visit

1. Make a plan. Think through what you hope to accomplish and how to go about reaching your goal. Consider your main message. What is your legislator's position on your issue, and what do you want them to do after the meeting? Consider whether having others join you in the meeting would help to convey your message. See "Tips for Effective Visits with Your Policy Maker."

2. Find a date and location. If you are meeting with a federal legislator, find out when your legislator is in your district, unless you plan to travel to Washington, DC. Check their website for current information about when they are on recess. If you plan to meet with a state or local legislator, be sure to check their website for details about their office location.

3. Request the meeting. First, call the local office (the one closest to you) and ask for the names of the legislator's scheduler and environmental assistant. Next, send an e-mail requesting a meeting to the attention of the scheduler. Indicate how flexible you are with the time of the meeting, as this will increase your chances of getting a meeting during busier days. A sample e-mail is provided below.

4. Follow up by phone. Within twenty-four hours of sending the e-mail, call the scheduler and confirm that they received it. If you have not heard back in three to four days, call the scheduler again and ask whether a meeting has been arranged. You can also use social media to contact the legislator if you haven't heard from the office.

Sample Meeting Request Email

ATTN: [Scheduler's Name]

Dear [Title and Last Name]:

I am writing to request a meeting with you and your aides on the subject of [your topic here.] [If appropriate, briefly mention any credentials or personal stake in the issue that might convince the scheduler to make you a priority.]

I wish to request a few minutes of your time to discuss [the immediate reasons for your request — e.g., developments in a piece of legislation] .

I will be available to meet with you anytime on [date(s)] and would be delighted to talk with you then about [the bill]. I would like to bring with me [list colleagues or other constituents if applicable], also from [your state/district].

I can be reached at the phone number(s) below and look forward to hearing from you soon.

Respectfully yours,

[Your Title and Full Name]
[Institution (if appropriate)]
[Address]
[Phone Numbers]

Tips for effective visits with your policy maker

Once you have set up your meeting, you'll need to prepare. Here are some tips to ensure you have a productive meeting:

1. Clarify your message. Before the meeting, formulate a clear message that you want to convey to your legislator. For instance, "Please play a leadership role in advancing policies to promote the widespread adoption of electric cars," or "Please vote for bills that will reduce global warming pollution."

2. Determine roles for participants. If more than one person is meeting with the legislator, designate a group leader to open and close the meeting and a different person to present each issue or message.

3. Practice for the meeting. It's always a good idea to run through what you intend to say before the meeting itself. If you are going with a group of people, have each person practice their part.

4. Dress nicely. Business attire is appropriate. If you are meeting in Washington, DC, business dress is required in the Capitol building.

5. Introduce yourself. Tell your legislator or staff person your name, where you are from, and that you are a constituent. If you represent an organization, note its name, where the group is located, and the size of its membership. If you are associated with a specific institution, identify it and your field of study (i.e., ecology). If you have any family, social, business, or political ties to the legislator, mention them as well. If relevant, thank the member for a good stand they recently took or mention that you voted for them. Thank them for taking the time to meet with you.

6. Take the initiative. State clearly and concisely what issue you want to discuss, what your position is, and what action you want the member to take. Follow this with facts about why they should take your position. Ask questions the legislator can respond to with "yes" or "no." Press politely for a commitment unless the member is clearly opposed to your position or to making a commitment.

7. Make a local connection. Stress how the issue will affect the legislator's district or state and, if possible, tell a personal story that highlights your experience with the issue and why you care about it.

8. Consider meeting with an aide. If your legislator is unavailable, you may end up meeting with their aide. While you should always ask for a meeting with the legislator, a meeting with the lead aide on your issue can be productive. The aide is the office expert on the issue and thus has influence with the legislator. If you are persistent and effective, you may be able to turn a first meeting with an aide into a long-term relationship with the office or a meeting directly with the legislator.

9. Have reasonable expectations. Don't expect your legislator to change a position after your twenty-minute meeting. You should view your meeting as one critical step among many to engage your legislator on the issue.

10. Bring a document to leave behind. Give the legislator a brief fact sheet (one to two pages) that outlines your position and explains why they should support it and what the bill does (if there is one).

11. Drop names. Mention any other organizations, important individuals, government officials, and legislators that support your position.

12. Don't answer what you don't know. It's okay not to know all the answers. Answer questions to the best of your ability. If you don't know an answer, admit it and offer to find out. This ensures you maintain credibility and allows an opportunity for a relevant follow-up to provide additional information.

13. Don't get discouraged. Members of the legislature are very busy and could be called out of the meeting — or not available at all — leaving you with the legislative aide who handles the issue. Don't let this discourage you. As noted above, meeting with a staff member can be equally or even more productive than meeting with the member. Be sure to ask the staff person to convey your views and legislative requests to their boss.

14. Stay on topic. The legislator may hijack the agenda or waste valuable time by bringing up unrelated issues. While it is important to be cordial and flexible, this is a meeting for you to relay your concerns to an elected official. Quickly acknowledge their issue and redirect the discussion back to the agenda. Don't let them take you off course for more than a moment.

15. Always follow up with a prompt thank-you e-mail. Reiterate your key points and any commitments the legislator made to you. Include any follow-up information you offered to provide.

Section II:
Corporate Activism

> scream and scream and scream until you break the back of
> one injustice
> ROSS GAY

Many of the tactics listed in this guide can be applied just as effectively to businesses and corporations to pressure them to adopt climate-friendly policies or to keep them from carrying out harmful practices. You can contact decision makers within companies to ask them to change the way they do business. You can use the media strategically (see section three): find out where the corporation you're trying to influence is headquartered or where employees are concentrated and follow the tips in this section to make waves within that media market. It matters to companies if their employees see bad publicity.

Some of the following tactics for targeting corporate policy will be most effective when you act as part of a larger group; see section four for more information.

LEVERAGE SOCIAL MEDIA

Bad publicity is bad for business, which is why large companies spend millions of dollars on their public image — their reputation — through advertising and public relations. Social-media campaigns are a simple way to create bad publicity for companies acting in bad faith. Some such campaigns have had serious consequences for businesses. If you're thinking of starting or joining a social-media campaign against a specific business, here are some tips to make the biggest splash:

Choose an issue that is in the news or is newsworthy — and easy to briefly explain. An example might be that ABC Fossil Fuel Corporation recently released a hypocritical ad about their support for environmental protections while they are dealing with the fallout of an oil spill.

Think about what you want the campaign to achieve. If you want more people to be aware of how the company has acted, a social-media campaign could be enough. If you want the company to do something specific, adding a phone call or e-mail campaign might achieve better results. Add instructions for further engagement to any social-media messages you're sending out, e.g., a phone number for the company's public relations office.

Be succinct. Most social-media platforms are not good at conveying nuance. There will always be more to the story. You must be selective and think of what dimension will resonate most.

Before you start your own campaign, think about how much influence you have. How many followers do you have on the platforms you use? Is there a group you are part of or can join with to amplify your message? Do you know an influential person on your platform who would care about your message enough to repost it? What will go viral is hard to predict, but having many people view your message is a great start.

Choose a simple and short hashtag that will stay in people's minds. It should communicate a lot while saying little. For example, #ExxonKnew references a campaign communicating that ExxonMobil's own scientists have known for decades how their company's products contribute to climate change, even as they attempt to sow doubt in the public sphere.

STRATEGICALLY EVALUATE YOUR INVESTMENTS

You probably don't own a majority share of Chevron or another corporation that profits from exacerbating climate change. But your retirement plan, your city or town, or your alma mater might have a substantial amount of investment money in portfolios that include major fossil-fuel corporations and other irresponsible actors. Some movements advocate for divesting from such investments. Alternatively, if your organization's share is large enough, you could opt to leverage that investment to effect change, becoming what's known as an "activist shareholder." Shareholders of publicly traded corporations are entitled to certain rights and can bring votes to other shareholders that force companies to make more socially responsible choices. For example, the New York State retirement fund and the Church of England, as shareholders in ExxonMobil, banded together successfully in 2017 to propose a resolution that requires the oil giant to report on how climate change will affect its bottom line.

Here are some tips to pressure corporations to act in line with your environmental values:

- If you have a retirement plan, trust fund, or other investment portfolio, check in with your account representative to find out where you are personally investing. With many 401(k) and 403(b) plans, you have the option to switch to socially responsible funds that do not invest money in fossil-fuel companies. You could also find out whether your provider has any interest in becoming an activist shareholder.

- If you belong to a union or another group with a large pension fund that has a significant investment in a polluting corporation, you can leverage your collective investment and become an activist shareholder in that way. Get in touch with your union or pension representatives to find out whether this is viable.

- Many cities and towns invest surplus or reserve funding. Check in with your municipal treasurer to learn what the investment portfolio for your community includes. Pressuring your city or town to divest from fossil-fuel companies or to be an activist shareholder would be a great project for a community-based group.

- Colleges and universities maintain large investment portfolios and are compelled to care about their alumni and student body's concerns; they solicit funding from the former and the latter become alumni. If you are a student or graduate, check the institutional investment policies for your college or university's endowment. Most institutions have a board of trustees responsible for handling investments; you can contact the board to find out what's in the portfolio. For inspiration, read up on Barnard College students' successful effort to convince their board of trustees to divest from fossil-fuel companies that promote climate-change denial.

USE YOUR PURCHASING POWER

Refusing to buy products or use services from environmentally unfriendly companies or those that support the fossil-fuel industry can be a powerful way to put your money where your values are. Boycotts can be organized or informal. A personal boycott may not make immediate waves, but you can talk about what you're doing and why you're doing it to friends and family and other social groups. Whether via social media or in-person conversations, you're likely to raise awareness and perhaps inspire others to take similar actions.

NOTE: It's nearly impossible to live in our world and not support harmful environmental policies, so please don't be wracked with guilt that you used one plastic straw or that you have to drive to work. Make environmentally friendly choices where you can, especially those that help reduce your own carbon footprint, while keeping your focus on systemic change. Take pride in your good choices and those you've encouraged others in your sphere to make.

PROTEST

Protests and rallies, sit-ins, and physical blockades can be effective means of changing corporate behavior. At the very least, they create bad publicity for businesses and tarnish their carefully cultivated public images. A powerful example can be found in the in-person Standing Rock protests against the Dakota Access Pipeline and the corresponding social-media protest #NoDAPL. A lot of forethought and strategy goes into such actions, and they are best planned and executed within like-minded groups. You should be mindful of your physical safety and the physical safety of all attendees, especially people of color and other marginalized people who are most often targeted for arrests and violence. When you participate, let your loved ones know that you are attending and listen to leaders from all involved communities to learn what steps are being taken to stay safe and unified. Read up on protests, sit-ins, and physical blockades online to be sure of your rights as a participant and for the best ways to get publicity and force corporate action, if you're an organizer.

Section III:
Connect with the Media

> Our melting, shifting, liquid world won't wait
> for manifesto or mandate, each
> warning a reckoning.
> MAURA DOOLEY

Because climate change is a dire issue, people need scientifically accurate and easily accessible information on how it will affect them, what they can do to forestall and prepare for its worst consequences, and how to reduce future impact. Considering how grave the threats of sea-level rise, higher temperatures, and worsening storms, droughts, and wildfires are, it's puzzling that media outlets don't prioritize coverage of climate change. Keep climate change in the news — the media is a powerful tool to amplify your message to a broad audience, from your own community to the decision makers you're trying to reach. What follows are some of the best ways to connect with and leverage the media.

WRITE A LETTER TO THE EDITOR

Writing a letter to the editor (LTE) of your local or regional newspaper is an effective and easy way to reach a large audience. LTEs are published on the editorial page, which is one of the most-read sections in any newspaper. Congressional staffers report that members of Congress keep a close eye on media coverage, including LTEs in their local papers so that they can keep up on issues of importance to their constituents. LTEs are also a good way to call attention to a corporate policy you'd like to encourage or change.

Even if your letter is not published, it can help to educate and persuade editors. The more letters they receive on a given topic, the more likely they are to dedicate more space in their newspaper to that issue — both on the editorial page and in news articles.

Tips for writing an effective LTE:

1. Respond to an article in the newspaper. The best letters are in response to a specific, recent article in the newspaper; many papers require this. A response to an editorial, op-ed, or front-page story has a greater chance of being printed. Begin by citing the original story by name, date, and author. Some papers occasionally print LTEs that note a lack of coverage on a specific issue. If this is the topic you are writing about, begin by stating your concern that the paper hasn't focused on this important topic.

2. Follow the paper's directions. Information on how and to whom to submit an LTE is usually found on the paper's letters page. Follow all guidelines to increase the likelihood that your letter will be printed. If you can't find the guidelines, call and ask how to submit a letter in response to an article.

3. Share your vantage point. If you are a doctor writing about a health issue or a Prius owner writing about hybrid cars, or if you live in a home powered by solar energy and are writing about energy issues, share that information up front.

4. Refer to the legislator or corporation you are trying to influence by name. If your letter includes a legislator's name, legislative staff is likely to give the legislator the letter to read. Corporations also monitor the media, especially in areas where they have offices or plants. Include the corporation's full name in your letter to get their attention.

5. Write the letter in your own words. Editors want letters to be original and from a reader.

6. Refute, advocate, and make a call to action. Most letters to the editor follow a standard format. Open your letter by refuting (or supporting) the claim made in the story the paper ran. Then use the next few sentences to back up your claims and advocate for your position. Try to focus on the positive. For example: *"According to a recent study, investments in renewable energy would bring over $200 million to our state and create 36,000 jobs by 2022."* Then wrap up by explaining what you think needs to happen now.

7. Include your contact information. Be sure to include your name, address, and daytime phone number; the paper will contact you before printing your letter.

Additional tips

Keep your letter concise and interesting. In general, letters should be under 200 words; 150 or fewer is best. Get to the main point in the first two sentences. Include interesting facts, relevant personal experience, and any local connections to the issue. If your letter is longer than 200 words, it will likely be edited or not printed.

Be timely. Respond to an article within two or three days of its publication.

Follow up. Get in touch with the legislator or corporation you're targeting. If your letter runs, forward it to the target with a brief, polite cover note.

WRITE AN OP-ED

Op-eds are unsolicited articles written by people not affiliated with news outlets — including business executives, scientists, schoolchildren, and engaged locals. Op-eds offer you a chance to get your viewpoint out into the world, potentially affecting public policy and gaining traction for an issue. They appear opposite the editorial page in most newspapers, often next to columns by syndicated writers.

It can be difficult to get an op-ed published because of limited space and a high number of submissions. You might consider other options first, as an op-ed takes more effort and time than, for example, a letter to the editor. If you do choose to go this route, here are some tips:

1. The beginning. Just like a good essay, op-eds have an introduction, body, and conclusion. The introduction should grab readers and encourage them to read on. Use timely references, vivid language, and metaphors. Try to limit the introductory paragraph to three sentences.

2. The middle. The body of the piece further develops your thesis, giving some background and context. Keep each paragraph short and focused, from three to five sentences, making one point in each paragraph. Every paragraph should tie back to the introduction and your overall thesis. Be sure not to get off track or follow tangents.

3. The end. The final paragraph should wrap up the piece and close strongly. Your conclusion should link to your introduction, carrying the same theme but adding something new. Use your conclusion to state your point or opinion. As the first sentence should grab the reader and make them want to continue to read, the last sentence should be memorable and make your overall point stick in the reader's mind.

4. Do some research first. Before you write, check with your local newspaper to find out the protocol for submitting opinion editorials. Call your paper and ask how they prefer to receive op-ed submissions (most accept them by e-mail), what the word limit is, to whose attention it should be sent, and if they require any supplemental information. Sending an op-ed without adhering to guidelines can keep even the best op-ed out of print.

5. Use a catchy headline that ties into the theme of your piece. The headline is what the reader sees first. Your headline should entice the reader, but remember that editors often change headlines.

6. Keep the op-ed short and to the point. Ideally, an op-ed should be 550–725 words, depending on guidelines.

7. Include personal information after the body of your op-ed: Include your name, university or organization, title, phone number, address. Many papers will not run a piece without confirming that you are the author of the piece.

8. Follow up. A few days after you submit your op-ed, you should place a follow-up call to the op-ed editor to check on their interest in running it.

MEET WITH AN EDITORIAL BOARD

An editorial board is a group of people at a newspaper who meet regularly to discuss news and opinion trends and what viewpoints their newspaper should take on issues. When an editorial unattributed to any one writer is published, it represents the board: the institutional opinion of that newspaper.

Editorial boards of newspapers are available and willing to meet with people who have something relevant to say about issues affecting their community — their purpose in publishing editorials is to recommend a plan of action, call public attention to an issue or program, or evaluate the actions of public officials or governments. If you would like to meet with an editorial board or writer, your message and the support you request should be consistent with those purposes.

Here are some tips for setting up and having a meeting with an editorial board:

1. Write a letter. To approach an editorial board, write a letter requesting a meeting; the letter should briefly describe the issue you are concerned about and why the editorial board should know your point of view on it. Follow up with a phone call or e-mail to see whether the board or an individual is interested in meeting with you.

2. Collect material and support. Prior to the meeting, collect concise, understandable, and useful background information and materials for the editorial board. Four to five different pieces of information are usually enough; more than that and the board may not read any of it. If possible, tie your presentation to a story recently covered by the newspaper or one that the newspaper knows is approaching. Be prepared to cite multiple local angles.

3. Be sure to follow up. After the meeting, send any additional information you promised along with a thank-you note.

GET MEDIA TO COVER YOUR EVENT

Getting media to come to your protest event isn't as hard as you might think. All you need is a short media advisory and the time to make a few phone calls.

1. Write your media advisory. A media advisory is a one-page notice about your event. It should contain five main components:

What. One sentence saying what your event is.

Where and when. The date, time, and location of your event.

Why. One to two paragraphs about why you are holding this event.

Who. Be sure at the end to include your name and contact information so that the reporter can call or e-mail you to ask for more details.

2. Send your advisory to your local media. You can usually find e-mail addresses for your local radio stations and newspapers on their websites. Look for the number for the main newsroom, too. If your event will look dramatic (i.e., it will be well attended, draw big names, or feature a significant action), don't forget to call your local television stations as well. Be sure to send your advisory out a few days ahead of time to give reporters time to get your event onto their schedules.

3. Make follow-up phone calls. The day after you send your advisory, you should follow up with the reporters you contacted. Review the advisory and have it in front of you when calling. Here's a sample script:

> Hi, I am [your name], a resident of [your town] and I'd like to let you know about a news event that might interest you. Do you have a second to talk? [If the reporter is on a deadline, he or she may not be able to speak to you just then. Ask them when a better time would be for you to call back. Then be sure to call them back at that time!]
> On [date and time], I will be/a group of concerned people will be [give the details of your event. Include what you're doing, why, and what you hope the outcome will be. *For example*: delivering hundreds of letters to John Doe, the local auto dealer who is one of ten dealership plaintiffs remaining in the controversial lawsuit against California's landmark law to reduce global-warming emissions from vehicles. We are urging that he drop the lawsuit because as customers we want to be able to buy clean cars.]
> You are welcome to join us. I have sent you a media advisory but would be happy to send it to you again. Are you interested in covering this event? Or is there someone else at your station/paper who might be more interested?

Section IV:
Find Your Power in Numbers

> But I feel like the saints are marching.
> They are singing a slow, deep, and beautiful song,
> Waiting for us to join in.
> LEE HERRICK

Working together with other individuals or groups toward a common goal will allow you to combine your assets for powerful action. Collaborations increase your chance for creating change by building strength in numbers, influence, and resources. Simply put: the more people you can involve in your action or event, the bigger difference you can make. For example, if your state government is debating a bill that would provide rebates for electric-car purchases, you'll make more of a difference if you join a group that works on this issue. Alone, you can make calls, write letters, or ask to meet with your representative. Together, you can organize a call day that will get hundreds of callers participating, schedule a group visit to the legislature to discuss or even testify on the issue, and get the credibility of an established organization behind your position. You'll get the broad benefits of being part of a community and the knowledge that you are not alone in your commitment to making a difference.

Common activities for collaboration include:

- Hosting a public event
- Getting local press coverage
- Fundraising
- Writing or sponsoring a published/public statement
- Working together on research projects or educational material
- Coordinating joint actions (e.g., call-in day, letters, meetings with legislators)
- Sharing news, best practices, and lessons learned.

Before taking group action, consider the strategic and personal value in working to ensure that there is equity in your group. Pollution and other environmental crises disproportionately impact the health and lives of marginalized people, including low-income communities and people of color. Do some research on local environmental justice or equity-based groups in your area as you consider organizing activities or events. What is already underway, and whose local leadership might you support to maximize benefits for those most vulnerable? Try to avoid duplicating the efforts of established groups in your area! Sometimes it is more important to join or support rather than to lead.

BE STRATEGIC

Review the following benefits of collaboration as you begin your planning. Which benefits of collective activism will help you reach your goals?

Widen your reach. Boost attendance at events, amplify publicity for activities, and bring together diverse voices to strengthen the message.

Set and accomplish bigger goals. Different interpretations, experiences, and expertise can combine for a comprehensive approach and a greater capacity to make change. Volunteers, funding, and strong relationships help make big goals achievable!

Build credibility. Different communities with shared concerns and a common message add credibility. Establishing your connections builds a positive reputation, shows solidarity, and can help boost your political clout and influence on policy makers.

Create community. By joining forces, you and others will recognize that you are a part of a larger movement. Especially in a challenging political climate, participants can be revitalized by a shared, inclusive space where ideas and support are flowing.

SCOUT FOR STRENGTHS

As you approach collaboration, identify the resources and skills needed to make maximum impact toward your goals. The following is a list of some key areas of strength that can be found within various groups and institutions:

1. **Within your personal network and affiliated groups.** Take stock of what like-minded members in your network are capable of, such as:

- Technology or computer skills: For the creation of websites and online event invitations, advertising through networking or social-media sites, and audiovisual needs.

- Scientific knowledge: Are there scientists in your group? Depending on their expertise, they might supply evidence to back up your positions. Science is still one of the most trusted and respected professional fields in the United States.

- Design or writing skills: To write press releases or articles, or to create flyers and fact sheets.

- Media contacts: Whether in print, radio, television, or online coverage, connections help to garner media attention.

- Influential connections: Connections that you or others have with businesses, celebrities, government officials, professional groups, or relevant organizations can be tapped to promote and add clout to your work.

- Language and cultural knowledge: Who can effectively organize, represent, or translate for the culturally diverse communities with stakes in the issue?

2. **In your own community.** Your neighborhood has a wealth of possible connections, from event locations to coorganizers, including:

- Local institutions: Some religious institutions, organized cultural groups, women's groups, community-serving organizations, or chapters of national organizations may bring additional perspectives and assets to the table.

- Popular community locations: Scope out possible sites to organize an event for the most attention and best reception possible. Keep in mind your target population and ultimate goal.

- Local like-minded, active businesses: Local businesses might donate to help your effort, publicize your activity, or leverage their clout.

- Local public websites: These are quick and easy tools for publicity and outreach.

3. **In your academic institution.** If you're a student, professor, or academic researcher, consider leveraging the resources and opportunities that academic institutions offer:

- Supportive faculty: Getting various academic sponsors or coorganizers can result in a well-rounded, well-funded, and well-attended activity. Consider reaching out to affiliated institutes, expert guest professors, affiliated associations, and other relevant schools.

- Campus-based media outlets: There should be many ways to reach your academic community for education or publicity.

- Small grants: Many schools have grant opportunities. Explore what options are available at your school and submit a proposal, aiming toward a fully funded activity.

HOW TO ORGANIZE A CALL-IN DAY

A call-in day can get the attention of your policy makers, while allowing you and your peers to easily take collective action. All offices of elected officials keep records of constituent calls and the issues raised. Coordinating a groundswell of people to call on a specific day will ensure that your congressional representatives take note of your issue and remind them they are accountable to their community.

Here are four steps for organizing a call-in day:

1. **Create a call-in script.** Callers will need the facts right in front of them. An effective script shouldn't be more than a few sentences. Remind your callers to:

- Tell your representative that you're a constituent — and share any affiliations with local institutions.

- Make a concrete request (e.g. "Vote no.").

- In a sentence or two, tell your representative why you care and what the implications are for the state and constituency.

- Thank them for their time.

- You can review "How to Contact Your Representatives" for more tips and details.

2. **Come up with an outreach strategy.** Take stock of the people and networks that may be interested in this issue, as well as any avenues where you could publicize your call-in day. To guide your planning, ask yourself:

Practical Tips for Positive Collaboration:

1. Make explicit agreements among your group before you start any projects together. Communication is key to a smooth and successful collaboration. Be clear on the "what, when, where, who, and how" of the efforts you seek to partner on.

2. Choose unifying issues. The most effective collaborations come together in response to a common issue and value. Make sure the development of group goals is a joint process rather than allowing one or two group representatives to decide on the goals and then inviting others to join.

3. Understand and respect each group's internal processes. There must be a balance between the goals and needs of the collaboration and of the individual groups/people, as well as a respect for groups' specific systems and policies. Make sure to take everyone's opinion and constraints into account and use diversity to spur discussion rather than divide.

4. Structure decision making and communication carefully. Finding consensus or alignment is very important when making decisions in partnerships. Listening and discussion are essential to finding common ground.

5. Distribute credit fairly. Recognize that contributions vary. Appreciate different contributions. Each partner will have something different to offer — volunteers, meeting space, funding, copying, publicity, leafleting, passing resolutions, or other resources. Each is important and warrants acknowledgment.

6. Celebrate and evaluate together. Celebrate together any accomplishments or successes. When reviewing the collaboration, ask yourselves: Did you achieve your goals? What lessons do you take away? Would you collaborate again on another project?

- Are there relevant active e-mail lists or social-media communities where you could send your call-in day information?
- If you're at a campus or part of a relevant community, could you set up a table to distribute scripts and connect with the public?
- Could you partner with other local organization chapters or school groups to promote the call-in day?
- Could hashtags or other digital materials help you spread the word online?

3. Promote and publicize. Once you know the people and avenues to reach out to, create a brief pitch as to why and how people should join the call-in day. To track call activity, you can create a collaborative document (e.g., a Google doc) or e-mail address for people to easily let you know that they called. Many hands make for lighter work — invite friends or colleagues to help you do this outreach.

4. Follow up. A few days after the call-in day, reach out to your elected officials to offer yourself as a resource. Offer more information on the issue and ask whether there is anything you can do to help them as they consider it. Also, reconnect with venues or people who participated to share how the activity went and give thanks for their involvement.

HOW TO HOST A PUBLIC EDUCATION EVENT

An event that brings people together to learn about an issue will build community and interest around your advocacy efforts. Creating a welcoming learning environment, reaching out to the right people, and effective follow-up are key.

1. Identify partners. Partnering with a community group is an excellent way to foster relationships, reach new people, and build power and influence.

- Begin by researching your topic and its stakeholders. Identify the people most affected by local climate change and invite them to take part.
- Look to community centers, churches, environmental or civic organizations, social and environmental justice groups, neighborhood associations, and more. Many of these groups can be found online.

- Be inclusive, and recognize that it may take time to develop trusting partnerships across communities.
- Define mutual goals for the meeting and your work together.
- Make the relationship reciprocal and beneficial to all involved.
- Let others contribute to the event development and encourage people to step into leadership and coordinator roles.
- Allow partners to play to their strengths and contribute whatever efforts make the most sense for them.

2. Select a location and plan event logistics. Make a ballpark estimate of the size of your event and choose a venue that will accommodate it.

- Look into local community spaces.
- If you are a student, faculty member, or employee of a local college, consider space on campus.
- Try to find a venue that is centrally located, accessible by public transportation, and has easy and ample parking.
- Consider accessibility; accommodate attendees with disabilities, those who speak different languages and may need interpreters, and those who may need childcare to attend.
- Provide accommodations for guest speakers, media, or other invited special guests.
- Ensure you are prepared for audiovisual needs and test technology in advance.
- Refreshments are always a perk. If funding is available, have the event catered (something as simple as pizza and salad). If the budget is limited, have a potluck or provide coffee, tea, and snacks. Reach out to local restaurants or delis to see whether they would consider donating food or discounting your order. Be willing to promote or advertise the restaurant to the audience (their potential customers) in exchange.
- Do not assume responsibility for everything. Discuss logistics with your partners and divide efforts by playing to each partner's strengths and connections.

3. Create an outreach plan for the event. Take stock of all the people and networks that you and your partners have identified and avenues where you can publicize the event. To guide your planning, try the following:

- Create an e-mail distribution list.
- Add relevant active e-mail lists or social-media communities where you could send your event information.
- Create digital and physical outreach materials (fliers, invitations) and plan where they will be distributed (at a tabling event, via a Facebook event invitation, on a local blog, in local cafés, and so on).
- Be as inclusive in outreach as you have been in organizing: reach out to those most affected by the issue at hand, not just technical experts and activists.

4. Promote and publicize. Coordinate with your partners to send out:

- An initial invitation about four to six weeks ahead of the event
- A reminder two weeks prior
- Another reminder early in the day of the event

When people RSVP, capture information useful to your campaign — for example, their names, addresses, e-mails, and experience with the issue. You could also collect this information at a registration table or by passing around a clipboard. Social media can be used before, during, and after the event to get attention and share information. Encourage people to use social media at the event to promote what is happening in real time.

5. Follow up. Stay in touch with the attendees after the event, and send updates on the issues addressed at the meeting. If there was a specific task or request of attendees, ask people to report on what they experienced or accomplished. Follow up within a week to share next steps with attendees. Share materials from the meeting — video, notes, photographs — and encourage others to do the same. You are building a community of people and groups working together for change.

Get Out There!

> The world asks of us
> only the strength we have and we give it.
> Then it asks more, and we give it.
> JANE HIRSHFIELD

You have the inspiration — the poems in this collection, together with your personal conviction — and a sense of the urgency of our climate crisis. Now you have a step-by-step guide to practical action. How will you use your voice to make a difference?

We can have a world that relies on clean, renewable energy rather than an addiction to fossil fuels. We can have farms that feed people and nourish the earth. We can have governments that protect the most vulnerable among us, including people living on the frontlines of climate change. We can care for animals and plants at risk of extinction. We can maintain and help restore our beautiful planet and provide a healthy standard of living for generations ahead.

These words may appear overly optimistic. They are not. Allow your imagination — sparked by the words in this book, perhaps, and by your vision of a just and sustainable life — to lead your work.

As His Holiness the Dalai Lama wrote in his foreword: "If we have the capacity to destroy the earth, so too, we have the capacity to protect it." This world is worth dreaming and working for. We are here, and we must move forward, together.

About the Editor

Elizabeth J. Coleman is a poet, environmental activist, public-interest attorney, and teacher of mindfulness. She is the author of two poetry collections, *The Fifth Generation* (Spuyten Duyvil Press, 2016) and *Proof* (Spuyten Duyvil Press, 2014), which was a finalist for the University of Wisconsin Press's Brittingham and Pollak prizes. She translated into French *Pythagoras in Love/Pythagore, Amoureux* (Folded Word Press, 2015), a bilingual sonnet collection. Her poems have been published in a number of journals and anthologies, and she is a vice president of the Poetry Society of America. A member of the New York, Georgia, and DC bars, Elizabeth runs Mindful Solutions LLC and is president of the Beatrice R. and Joseph A. Coleman Foundation. In *Here,* Elizabeth brings together her love for poetry, for justice, and for our planet.

Contributors

Poets

Chris Abani has published both poetry and fiction, including *The Secret History of Las Vegas, Sanctificum,* and *Feed Me the Sun: Collected Long Poems.* He is the recipient of the PEN Center USA Freedom to Write Award, the Prince Claus Award, a Lannan Literary Fellowship, a California Book Award, a Hurston/Wright Legacy Award, and a Guggenheim Fellowship. Born in Nigeria, he lives in Chicago, where he is Board of Trustees Professor of English at Northwestern University.

Julia Alvarez is the author of *How the García Girls Lost Their Accents,* winner of the PEN Oakland/Josephine Miles Literary Award; *In the Time of the Butterflies;* and *Yo!,* which was selected as a notable book by the American Library Association. She is also the recipient of the Lamont Prize from the Academy of American Poets, the Fitzgerald Award for Achievement in American Literature, and the Hispanic Heritage Award in Literature. She is a writer-in-residence emerita at Middlebury College.

Francisco Aragón, the son of Nicaraguan immigrants, is the author of *Glow of Our Sweat* and *Puerta del Sol,* as well as the editor of *The Wind Shifts: New Latino Poetry. After Rubén,* his third book, is forthcoming from Red Hen Press. He is the director of Letras Latinas, the literary initiative at the University of Notre Dame's Institute for Latino Studies. He divides his time between Notre Dame, Indiana, and Arlington, Virginia.

Betye Arrastia-Nowak is a student in upstate New York. She was a member of Kite's Nest's Social Justice Leadership Academy.

James Arthur is the author of *Charms Against Lightning.* A second collection, *The Suicide's Son,* is forthcoming from Véhicule Press. He has received a Discovery/The Nation Prize, a Hodder Fellowship, and a Stegner Fellowship. He lives in Baltimore, Maryland, where he teaches in The Writing Seminars at Johns Hopkins University.

Fadhil Assultani is an Iraqi poet, translator, and journalist. He has lived in London since 1994 and works as an editor of the cultural department at the daily London-based newspaper *Asharq Al-Awsat.* He has published several books of poetry and translation. Some of his poems have been translated into German, Spanish, Kurdish, Persian, and English.

Margaret Atwood is the author of more than fifty books of fiction, poetry, and critical essays. Her latest book of short stories is *Stone Mattress: Nine Tales.* Her most recent novel, *The Heart Goes Last,* was published in September 2015. Other recent works include the MaddAddam trilogy — the Giller and Booker prize–nominated *Oryx and Crake, The Year of the Flood,* and *MaddAddam. The Door* is her latest volume of poetry. In 2017, Atwood was awarded with the Peace Prize of the German Book Trade, the Franz Kafka International Literary Prize, and the PEN Center USA Lifetime Achievement Award. She lives in Toronto with writer Graeme Gibson.

Gabeba Baderoon is the author of *The History of Intimacy, A Hundred Silences,* and *The Dream in the Next Body.* Her poems also appear as songs on the CD *Out of Time,* by Robert Stone. Baderoon is the recipient of the DaimlerChrysler Award for South African Poetry and the Best Nonfiction Monograph Award from the National Institute for the Humanities and Social Sciences for her study *Regarding Muslims: From Slavery to Post-Apartheid.* She codirects the African Feminist Initiative at Pennsylvania State University, where she is an associate professor of women's, gender, and sexuality studies and African studies.

David Baker's collections of poetry include *Changeable Thunder, Midwest Eclogue, Never-Ending Birds, Scavenger Loop,* and the forthcoming *Swift: New and Selected Poems.* He is currently a professor of English and the Thomas B. Fordham Chair in Creative Writing at Denison University, as well as the editor of the *Kenyon Review.*

Griffon Bannon wrote "How to Be a Hawk" at age eleven. The poem was the poetry grand prize winner for River of Words 2015.

Jesús J. Barquet was born in Havana in 1953. He won the Letras de Oro Prize for *Consagración de La Habana* and the Lourdes Casal Prize for *Escrituras poéticas de una nación* (1998). Among his books of poetry are *Sagradas herejías, Aguja de diversos, Sin fecha de extinción, Los viajes venturosos* (Venturous Journeys), and the compilation *Cuerpos del delirio.* He has served as editor in chief of La Mirada publishing house since 2014.

Julia Beckwith's poem "every sunrise is a sunset, somewhere" was a Helen Creeley Student Poetry Prize semifinalist in 2017.

Wendell Berry is the first living writer to be inducted into the Kentucky Writers Hall of Fame. He is the author of more than thirty books of poetry, essays, and fiction, including *Given, A World Lost,* and *Remembering.* Among his honors and awards are fellowships from the Guggenheim and Rockefeller foundations, a Lannan Foundation Award, and a grant from the National Endowment for the Arts. He lives in Port Royal, Kentucky, where he has maintained a farm for over forty years.

Catriona Bolt is a student of English language and literature at Lincoln College. In 2013 she was a Foyle Young Poet of the Year and was also highly commended in the Timothy Corsellis Prize in 2014. She has been published by the *Isis* and *Cadaverine.*

Marina Boroditskaya is the author of three books of poetry, twelve books of poems for children, and numerous translations of poems and fairy tales from English to Russian. Marina has received several prizes for poetry and translation, including the prestigious Korney Chukovsky Prize for children's poetry. She lives in Russia.

Annie Boutelle is the author of *Thistle and Rose: A Study of Hugh MacDiarmid's Poetry* and scholarly and popular articles on a wide range of topics. Her collections of poems include *Becoming Bone,* based on the life of nineteenth-century American poet Celia Thaxter, and *Nest of Thistles,* which focuses on her Scottish childhood and was the winner of the Samuel French Morse Poetry Prize.

Kamau Brathwaite is the author of *The Lazarus Poems, Elegguas,* and *Ancestors,* among other collections of poetry. He is the recipient of a Neustadt International Prize for

Literature, the Casa de Las Américas Prize for poetry and for literary criticism, and fellowships from the Guggenheim Foundation, the Fulbright Foundation, and the Ford Foundation. He divides his time between Barbados and New York City, where he is a professor of comparative literature at New York University.

Traci Brimhall is the author of *Saudade*; *Our Lady of the Ruins*, winner of the Barnard Women Poets Prize; *Rookery*, winner of the Crab Orchard Series in Poetry First Book award; and the forthcoming *Come the Slumberless to the Land of Nod*. She has also been awarded a Jane Geske Award from *Prairie Schooner* and fellowships from the National Endowment for the Arts and Bread Loaf, among others. She lives in Manhattan, Kansas, where she is an associate professor of creative writing at Kansas State University.

Robert Bringhurst's *Selected Poems* was published by Copper Canyon Press in the United States and by Jonathan Cape in London. He is also the author of *A Story as Sharp as a Knife: The Classical Haida Mythtellers and Their World* and *The Elements of Typographic Style*. He is a lifelong student of Native American languages and has published extensive translations from Haida and Navajo. His most recent book is *Learning to Die*, coauthored with Jan Zwicky.

Lauryn Brown wrote "Voice" at age fifteen while attending North Polk High School in Polk City, Iowa.

Nickole Brown is the author of *Fanny Says*. She lives in Asheville, North Carolina, where she is the editor for the Marie Alexander Poetry Series and teaches periodically at the Sewanee School of Letters MFA program, the Great Smokies Writing Program at University of North Carolina Asheville, and the Hindman Settlement School.

John Calderazzo is the author of many stories, essays, poems, and books, including *Rising Fire: Volcanoes and Our Inner Lives*, *101 Questions about Volcanoes*, and *Writing from Scratch: Freelancing*. He is a professor of English, Emeritus, at Colorado State University and also teaches scientists to use story-telling skills to communicate better with the public and with decision makers.

Wiñay Mallki, or Fredy Chicangana, is the author of *Taquinam Cuyaypa manchachipak huañuyman*, *Kinde tutamanta yaravi nina*, and *Ñuka Yanacona, shimi yuyaipas*. He is the recipient of the National University of Colombia Humanity and the Word Prize and the Nosside de Poesía Global Multilingüe Prize in Italy. A member of the Yanakuna Mitmak Nation in Sur-Oriente del Cauca, Colombia, he is involved in several initiatives to preserve and promote Yanakuna identity and spaces sacred to the Yanakuna.

Mary Anne Clark studies English at Merton College, Oxford, where she won the 2016 Newdigate Prize. She is also the recipient of the Foyle Young Poets of the Year Award, the Cape Farewell and Edith Sitwell prizes from the Poetry Society's Young Poets' Network, and the Ledbury and Basil Bunting awards. Her poems have appeared in *ASH*, *The Mays*, and two anthologies from the Emma Press.

Elizabeth J. Coleman, editor of *Here: Poems for the Planet*, is the author of *The Fifth Generation* and *Proof*, which was a finalist for the Brittingham and Pollak prizes. She has written two chapbooks, *Let My Ears Be Open* and *The Saint of Lost Things*, and translated into French the bilingual sonnet collection *Pythagoras in Love/Pythagore, Amoureux*. Coleman's poetry has appeared in numerous anthologies and journals. In addition, she is an attorney, mindfulness teacher, guitarist, and environmental activist.

Michaela Coplen was a National Student Poet in 2013. She has interned with the US Army, the UK Cabinet Office, the United States Agency for International Development in Jordan and served as editor in chief for Scholastic's award-winning anthology *The Best Teen Writing of 2015*. She is a graduate student at the University of Oxford, where she is pursuing an MPhil in international relations.

Ryan P. Corey wrote "Sparkle Rock" in first grade at Setauket Elementary School in Setauket, New York.

Lucha Corpi is a renowned poet, novelist, and children's book author. Her mystery novels include *Death at Solstice, Eulogy for a Brown Angel*, and *Cactus Blood*. She has published two poetry collections, *Palabras de mediodía* (Noon Words) and *Variaciones sobre una tempestad* (Variations on a Storm), two children's books, and a memoir, *Confessions of a Book Burner: Personal Essays and Stories*. Corpi is the recipient of numerous awards and citations, including a National Endowment for the Arts Fellowship and the PEN Oakland/Josephine Miles Literary Award. She was a tenured teacher in the Oakland Public Schools Neighborhood Centers Program for over thirty years.

Sapardi Djoko Damono is widely regarded as the pioneer of lyric poetry in Indonesia. His first collection, *duka-Mu Abadi* (Your Eternal Sorrow), was released in 1969. Sapardi has also completed a number of translations of literary works into Indonesian.

Chekwube O. Danladi is the author of the chapbook *Take Me Back* and has been featured in *Apogee, Callaloo, West Branch, Black Warrior Review,* and elsewhere. She is the recipient of the 2016 Brunel International African Poetry Prize and is currently the Jay C. and Ruth Halls Poetry Fellow at the Wisconsin Institute for Creative Writing.

Alfonso D'Aquino is the author of six books of poetry, including *Basilisco, Víbora Breve,* and *Naranja Verde*. At the age of twenty-two, he was awarded the Carlos Pellicer Poetry Prize. He lives and works as an editor and teacher in Coyoacán, México.

Kyle Dargan is the author of five collections of poetry, including *The Listening*, which won the 2003 Cave Canem Poetry Prize, and *Bouquet of Hungers*, which was awarded the 2008 Hurston/Wright Legacy Award in poetry. His most recent collection is *Anagnorisis*. He lives in Washington, DC, where he is the assistant director of creative writing and an associate professor of literature at American University.

Corinna Davidson wrote "Rules of the Mouse" while attending Annie Wright Day School.

Kwame Dawes is the author of numerous books. His poetry collections include *Wisteria: Poems from the Swamp Country, Impossible Flying, Back of Mount Peace, Hope's Hospice, Wheels, Duppy Conqueror: New and Selected Poems,* and *City of Bones: A Testament*. His honors and awards include the Forward Prize for Poetry for his first book, *Progeny of Air*; the Hollis Summers Poetry Prize; a Pushcart Prize; the Hurston/Wright Legacy Award; the Barnes and Noble Writers for Writers Award; and a Guggenheim

Foundation fellowship.

Natalie Diaz is Mojave and an enrolled member of the Gila River Indian tribe. Her first poetry collection, *When My Brother Was an Aztec*, was published by Copper Canyon Press. She is a MacArthur Fellow, Lannan Literary Fellow, and a Native Arts Council Foundation Artist Fellow. Diaz is the Maxine and Jonathan Marshall Chair in Modern and Contemporary Poetry at Arizona State University.

Maura Dooley is the author of several collections published by Bloodaxe Books, including *The Silvering*; *Life Under Water*, which was short-listed for the T.S. Eliot Prize; *Sound Barrier: Poems 1982–2002*; and *Kissing a Bone*, also short-listed for the T.S. Eliot Prize. She lives in London, where she is a freelance writer and lectures at Goldsmiths College.

Tishani Doshi is the author of *The Pleasure Seekers*, which was short-listed for the Hindu Best Fiction Award and long-listed for the Orange Prize and the International Dublin Literary Award; *Countries of the Body*, which won a Forward Prize for Best First Collection; *Everything Begins Elsewhere*, and other collections. Her third collection is *Girls Are Coming Out of the Woods*. She lives in Tamil Nadu, India.

Mark Doty is the author of *My Alexandria*, winner of the National Poetry Series, a National Book Critics Circle Award, a Los Angeles Times Book Prize, and a T.S. Eliot Prize; *Dog Years*, which won a Lambda Literary Award and Stonewall Book Award; and *Fire to Fire: New and Selected Poems*, which received the National Book Award for Poetry. A former chancellor of the Academy of American Poets, he is a distinguished professor of English at Rutgers University.

Camille T. Dungy is the author of four collections of poetry, most recently *Trophic Cascade*, winner of the Colorado Book Award, as well as a collection of personal essays, *Guidebook to Relative Strangers*. She is also the recipient of two Northern California Book Awards, a California Book Award silver medal, two NAACP Image Award nominations, two Hurston/Wright Legacy Award nominations, fellowships from the Sustainable Arts Foundation, and fellowships from the National Endowment for the Arts in both poetry and prose. She is currently a professor in the English department at Colorado State University. She lives in Fort Collins, Colorado, with her husband and child.

Sharif S. Elmusa is a scholar, poet, and translator. In addition to his many academic publications on the culture and politics of the environment, he is coeditor of the anthology *Grape Leaves: A Century of Arab-American Poetry* and author of the poetry collection *Flawed Landscape*. His poetry, essays, and translations from Arabic appear widely in anthologies, in print magazines in the US and internationally, and on the web. Elmusa is the recipient of Fulbright and Yale University Coca-Cola fellowships. He taught at the American University in Cairo, Egypt, for many years, at Georgetown University, Qatar, and at Yale University. Elmusa is Palestinian by birth and American by citizenship.

Vievee Francis is the author of *Forest Primeval*, winner of the 2017 Kingsley Tufts Award; *Horse in the Dark*, winner of the Cave Canem Northwestern University Press Poetry Prize; and *Blue-Tail Fly*. She is an associate professor at Dartmouth College and an associate editor for *Callaloo*.

Katie Friedman wrote "Haiku" at age thirteen while attending Lakeside Middle School in Seattle, Washington.

Ross Gay is the author of *Catalog of Unabashed Gratitude*, winner of the National Book Critics Circle Award and the Kingsley Tufts Poetry Award, among others; *Bringing the Shovel Down*; and *Against Which*. He has received fellowships from Radcliffe College and the Guggenheim Foundation and coauthored a chapbook, *Lace and Pyrite: Letters from Two Gardens*. He has a forthcoming book, *The Book of Delights*, and is a professor of English at Indiana University.

Mordechai Geldman was born in Munich in 1946 and arrived in Israel in 1949. An art critic, artist, author, poet, and psychotherapist, Geldman has published fourteen volumes of poetry and five essay collections and is the recipient of the Chomsky Prize for Poetry, the Brenner Prize, the Yehuda Amichai Prize for Hebrew Poetry, the Prime Minister's Prize for Hebrew Writers, and the Bialik Prize in Literature. His work has been translated into English, Arabic, Czech, French, Greek, German, Italian, Polish, Romanian, Serbo-Croatian, Spanish, Japanese, Portuguese, and Vietnamese. He lives and works in Tel Aviv.

Danielle Legros Georges is the current Poet Laureate of Boston. She is the author of *The Dear Remote Nearness of You*, winner of the New England Poetry Club's Sheila Margaret Motton Book Prize, and *Maroon*, and is the editor of *City of Notions: An Anthology of Contemporary Boston Poems*. She is a professor of creative writing at Lesley University and a faculty member of the Joiner Institute Summer Writers' Workshop at the University of Massachusetts, Boston. Her honors include fellowships from the Massachusetts Cultural Council, the Boston Foundation, and the Black Metropolis Research Consortium.

Nikki Giovanni is the author of numerous children's books and poetry collections, including *A Good Cry*, *Chasing Utopia: A Hybrid*, *Bicycles: Love Poems*, and *Black Judgement*. Her honors include a fellowship from the National Endowment for the Arts, the Reverend Martin Luther King Jr. Award for Dedication and Commitment to Service, seven NAACP Image Awards for Literature, and the Langston Hughes Award for Distinguished Contributions to Arts and Letters. She is currently University Distinguished Professor at Virginia Tech, where she has taught since 1987.

Rigoberto González is the author of seventeen books of poetry and prose, most recently the memoir *What Drowns the Flowers in Your Mouth*. His awards include fellowships from the Guggenheim Foundation, the National Endowment for the Arts, New York Foundation for the Arts, and USA Rolón; the American Book Award from the Before Columbus Foundation; the Lenore Marshall Poetry Prize from the Academy of American Poets; and the Shelley Memorial Award from the Poetry Society of America. A critic at large for the *Los Angeles Times,* he sits on the board of trustees of the Association of Writers and Writing Programs (AWP) and is currently a professor of English at Rutgers-Newark, the State University of New Jersey.

Lorna Goodison is the Poet Laureate of Jamaica and is the recipient of numerous prizes for her work, including the 2018 Windham Campbell Prize for Poetry from Yale University. She is the author of twelve collections of poetry, three collections of short stories, an award-winning memoir, and a collection of essays. Her work has been included in the major anthologies and collections of contemporary poetry published in the United States, Europe, and the West Indies over the past thirty years, including the *Norton Anthology of Modern and Contemporary Poetry* as well as the *HarperCollins World Reader,* the *Vintage Book of Contemporary World Poetry,* the *Norton Anthology of World Masterpieces,* and *Longman Masters of British Literature.* She is Professor Emerita in the Department of English at the Center for Afroamerican and African Studies at the University of Michigan.

Joy Goswami is an Indian poet. He writes in Bengali and is widely considered to be one of the most important Bengali poets of his generation. His books include *Ghumiyecho Jhaupata* and *Jara Brishhtite Bhijechchhilo,* both winners of the prestigious Ananda Purashkar. In 1997 he won the West Bengal Academy Award for *Bojro Bidyut Bharti Khata* and has also received the Sahitya Akademi award for his book *Paagli Tomar Songe.*

Rachel Eliza Griffiths is the author of *Mule & Pear,* which was selected for the 2012 Inaugural Poetry Award by the Black Caucus American Library Association; *Lighting the Shadow*; and *The Requited Distance,* among others. She has also received fellowships from Cave Canem, Kimbilio, Yaddo, and the Provincetown Fine Arts Work Center. She lives in New York City, where she teaches creative writing at Sarah Lawrence College.

Jennifer Grotz is the author of *Window Left Open*; *The Needle,* which was named the 2012 Best Book of Poetry by the Texas Institute of Letters; and *Cusp,* winner of the Katharine Bakeless Nason Poetry Prize. She is the recipient of numerous awards, including the Rona Jaffe Foundation Writers' Award and fellowships from the National Endowment for the Arts and the Guggenheim Foundation. Director of the Bread Loaf Writers' Conferences, she teaches at the University of Rochester.

Paul Guest is the author of five collections of poems — *Because Everything Is Terrible, My Index of Slightly Horrifying Knowledge, Notes for My Body Double, Exit Interview: Poems,* and *The Resurrection of the Body and the Ruin of the World* — and a memoir, *One More Theory about Happiness.* His honors and awards include a Whiting Award and a Guggenheim Foundation Fellowship. He lives in Charlottesville, Virginia, where he is an assistant professor of creative writing at the University of Virginia.

Noa Gur-Arie wrote "Dolbear's Law" at age sixteen while attending Bethesda-Chevy Chase High School in Bethesda, Maryland.

Hadley, the author of "The Mighty Guardian," attended the First Baptist Christian Academy, Lincoln County, Missouri.

Kimiko Hahn is the author of nine books of poetry, including *The Artist's Daughter, The Narrow Road to the Interior, Toxic Flora,* and *Brain Fever.* Hahn is the winner of the PEN/Voelcker Award for Poetry, the American Book Award, and the Shelley Memorial Award from the Poetry Society of America. She has also been awarded fellowships from the New York Foundation for the Arts, the Guggenheim Foundation, and the National Endowment for the Arts. Hahn teaches in the MFA program at Queens College. In 2016, she was elected president of the Poetry Society of America.

Kendra Hamilton is the author of *The Goddess of Gumbo* and a contributor to the anthologies *Bush Rush the Page: A Def Poetry Jam*, *The Ringing Ear: Black Poets Lean South*, and *Black Nature: Centuries of African American Nature Poetry*. Her work has been featured in journals such as *Callaloo, The Southern Review,* and *Mississippi Quarterly;* her work of literary criticism, *Romancing the Gullah,* is forthcoming from University of Georgia Press. She teaches African American and Southern literature and directs the Southern studies program at Presbyterian College in Clinton, South Carolina.

Joy Harjo has received many honors, including the lifetime achievement award from the Native Writers Circle of the Americas, the PEN Oakland/Josephine Miles Literary Award, the Wallace Stevens Award from the Academy of American Poets, the William Carlos Williams Award from the Poetry Society of America, and the American Indian Distinguished Achievement in the Arts Award. In 2017 she was awarded the Ruth Lilly Poetry Prize. Harjo's memoir, *Crazy Brave,* won the American Book Award and the 2013 PEN Center USA prize for creative nonfiction.

David Hart lives in Britain. He was born and grew up in Aberystwyth and now lives in Birmingham. His poems have been widely published in magazines and anthologies and his books and pamphlets include *Setting the Poem to Words, Crag Inspector (A Poem of Bardsey Island), Running Out, The Titanic Café Closes Its Doors and Hits the Rocks,* and *Library Inspector*.

Robert Hass served as Poet Laureate of the United States from 1995 to 1997. He is the author of *Time and Materials: Poems 1997–2005,* which received a National Book Award and a Pulitzer Prize; *Twentieth Century Pleasures: Prose on Poetry,* which received a National Book Critics Circle Award; and *Field Guide,* which received a Yale Series of Younger Poets Award, among other works. He lives in California with his wife and is Distinguished Professor in Poetry and Poetics at the University of California, Berkeley.

Louise Herlin is the author of collections such as *Synchronies, Les oiseaux de Méryon,* and *Le poème inachevé*. Born in Cairo, she now lives in Paris, France.

Lee Herrick is a Fresno Poet Laureate Emeritus. He is the author of *Scar and Flower, Gardening Secrets of the Dead,* and *This Many Miles from Desire*. He lives with his daughter and wife in Fresno, California, where he teaches at Fresno City College and in the MFA program at Sierra Nevada College.

Bob Hicok is the author of *Hold,* his ninth book. A Guggenheim and two-time National Endowment for the Arts fellow, he received the Bobbitt Prize from the Library of Congress for *This Clumsy Living*. Twice a finalist for the National Book Critics Circle Award, he has won eight Pushcart Prizes and been included in nine volumes of *Best American Poetry*.

Brenda Hillman is the author of ten collections from Wesleyan University Press, most recently *Extra Hidden Life, among the Days, Seasonal Works with Letters on Fire,* and *Practical Water*. Her fourth book, *Bright Existence,* was a finalist for the Pulitzer Prize. Other collections have received the Los Angeles Times Book Prize and the William Carlos Williams Prize. Hillman recently cotranslated *At Your Feet, the Poems of Ana Cristina Cesar*.

She lives in the Bay Area with her husband, Robert Hass, and is Olivia Filippi Professor of Poetry at St. Mary's College in Moraga, California.

Krassin Himmirsky is a poet and former career diplomat. He has published multiple works of poetry and fiction and has taught at Sofia University, the University of National and World Economy, the New Bulgarian University, Shumen University, and the American University in Bulgaria.

Jane Hirshfield is the author of *The Beauty: Poems*, long-listed for the National Book Award, and *Given Sugar, Given Salt*, a finalist for the National Book Critics Circle Award, among other books of poems, as well as two now-classic collections of essays, *Ten Windows* and *Nine Gates*, and four books collecting and cotranslating the work of world poets from the past. Her honors include fellowships from the Guggenheim Foundation, the National Endowment for the Arts, the Rockefeller Foundation, and the Academy of American Poets. She served as a chancellor of the Academy of American Poets from 2012 to 2018 and is the founder of Poets for Science. She lives in the San Francisco Bay Area.

Huang Canran was born in 1963 in a remote village in Quanzhou, Fujian. From 1990 to 2014, he worked as an international news translator for the Hong Kong newspaper *Ta Kung Pao*. His poetry collections include *Meditation Beside a Swimming Pool, My Soul,* and *Book of Wonders*. In addition to his work as poet, he is widely known for his prolific literary translations into Chinese, largely poetry and poetry criticism. Notable among these are his renderings of C.P. Cavafy, César Vallejo, Czesław Miłosz, Joseph Brodsky, and Seamus Heaney.

David Huerta is the author of *Incurable, Cuaderno de noviembre,* and *Versión,* among others books of poetry. He is the recipient of numerous awards, including the Carlos Pellicer Poetry Prize and the Xavier Villaurrutia Award, as well as Mexico's National Prize for Literature (2015) and fellowships from the Mexican Writers' Center and the Guggenheim Foundation. He was an editor of Fondo de Cultura Económica, writes for the newspaper *El Universal,* and teaches literature at the Universidad Autónoma de México.

Katerina Iliopoulou is the author of four poetry books (most recently *Every Place Once, and Completely*) and a book of short stories. Her published translations include the work of Sylvia Plath and Walt Whitman. She is chief editor of the poetry magazine *FRMK* and of the bilingual platform greekpoetrynow.com. She lives in Athens, Greece.

Richard Jackson is the author of twenty-five books, including fifteen books of poems, among them *Resonance, Out of Place,* and *Broken Horizons*. He was awarded the Order of Freedom Medal by the president of Slovenia and has received the AWP George Garrett Award as well as Guggenheim, Fulbright, Witter Bynner, National Endowment for the Arts, and National Endowment for the Humanities fellowships. He teaches creative writing, poetry, and humanities at the University of Tennessee at Chattanooga.

Joan Naviyuk Kane is the author of *Milk Black Carbon*; *Hyperboreal,* chosen for the Donald Hall Prize for Poetry; *The Cormorant Hunter's Wife*; and other poetry and prose collections. She has also received a Whiting Award and fellowships from the Native Arts and

Cultures Foundation, the Rasmuson Foundation, and the Alaska State Council on the Arts. She is Inupiaq with family from King Island (Ugiuvak) and Mary's Igloo, Alaska. She lives in Anchorage, where she teaches at the Institute of American Indian Arts.

Jaan Kaplinski is the author of *The Wandering Border, Seesama jõgi,* and *Õhtu toob tagasi kõik,* among others. He has been awarded the Baltic Assembly Prize for Literature, the Arts, and Science. He has worked at the Tallinn Botanic Garden, the University of Tartu, as a member of the parliament, and as a writer-in-residence at Aberystwyth University in Wales.

Laura Kasischke is the author of *Space, In Chains,* winner of the National Book Critics Circle Award; *The Life Before Her Eyes; White Bird in a Blizzard;* and other works. She has received several Pushcart Prizes, the Juniper Prize for Poetry, and fellowships from the National Endowment for the Arts and the Guggenheim Foundation. She lives in Chelsea, Michigan, and teaches at the University of Michigan.

Olivia Keener's work has received honors and been published by the Philadelphia Alumni Writers House at Franklin & Marshall College as well as in *Poetry Paths: Poetry and Public Art in Lancaster, Pennsylvania, Volume V* and *Conserving the Land.*

Esma'il Kho'i is the author of over thirty books in Farsi, with selections in English translation, including *Outlandia: Songs of Exile* and *Edges of Poetry: Selected Poetry.* A prominent voice of the Iranian diaspora, he lives in the United Kingdom.

David Kirby is the author of more than thirty books, including *The Ha-Ha,* which was short-listed for the Griffin Poetry Prize, and *The House on Boulevard Street: New and Selected Poems,* which was a finalist for the National Book Award and winner of the Florida Book Award and the Southern Independent Booksellers Alliance Award. He has also received several Pushcart Prizes and fellowships from the Guggenheim Foundation and the National Endowment for the Arts. He lives in Tallahassee, Florida, where he teaches at Florida State University.

Chip Livingston is a Creek poet, editor, translator, and author of *Owls Don't Have to Mean Death, Naming Ceremony, Crow-Blue, Crow-Black,* and *Museum of False Starts: Poems.* His honors include awards from the Native Writers' Circle of the Americas and Wordcraft Circle of Native Writers and Storytellers and three nominations for a Pushcart Prize. He lives in Montevideo, Uruguay, and teaches in the low-residency MFA program at the Institute of American Indian Arts.

Valdemar á Løgmansbø is the author of *Mín jólabók 2014* and *Svartideyði og aðrar spøkilsissøgur.* Løgmansbø is a songwriter and composer as well as a poet. He lives in Miðvágur, Vágar, Faroe Islands.

Anne Marie Macari is the author of five books of poems, most recently *Red Deer* and the forthcoming *Heaven Beneath.* Her first book, *Ivory Cradle,* won the APR/ Honickman Book Prize in 2000. She lives in New York City.

Salgado Maranhão is the author of *Blood of the Sun* and *Tiger Fur* as well as many other works. He has received every major literary award in Brazil, including the Brazilian PEN Club Prize for his work *O mapa da tribo*, the poetry award from the Brazilian Academy of Letters, and the Jabuti Award.

Jamaal May is the author of *The Big Book of Exit Strategies* and *Hum*, which received a Beatrice Hawley Award and was an American Library Association Notable Book. He is also the recipient of a Spirit of Detroit Award, the Wood Prize from *Poetry*, *Indiana Review*'s Poetry Prize, and fellowships from the Stadler Center, *Kenyon Review*, and the Civitella Ranieri Foundation in Italy. He lives in Hamtramck, Michigan, where he codirects OW! Arts, a publisher of chapbooks.

From Jamaica, **Shara McCallum** is the author of five books of poetry published in the United States and the United Kingdom. Most recently is *Madwoman*, winner of the 2018 OCM Bocas Poetry Prize for Caribbean Literature and the 2018 Sheila Margaret Motton Book Prize. Her work has been widely published in the US, the Caribbean, and Europe; has been translated into several languages; and has received such recognition as a Witter Bynner Fellowship from the Library of Congress and a Poetry Fellowship from the National Endowment for the Arts. From 2003–17 she directed the Stadler Center for Poetry and is now a Liberal Arts Professor of English at Penn State University.

Rose McLarney is the author of *Its Day Being Gone*, winner of the National Poetry Series, and *The Always Broken Plates of Mountains*. A third collection, *Forage*, is forthcoming. She has been awarded fellowships from Bread Loaf, MacDowell Colony, Sewanee, Warren Wilson College's MFA program, and the Dartmouth poet-in-residence program at the Frost Place. She is associate professor of creative writing at Auburn University and coeditor of *Southern Humanities Review*.

Jane Mead is the author of five poetry collections, including *World of Made and Unmade*, which was long-listed for the National Book Award; *Money Money Money Water Water Water*; and *The Usable Field*. She is the recipient of awards and fellowships from the Lannan, Whiting, and Guggenheim foundations. She lives on and manages her family's ranch in northern California.

Pablo Medina is the author of *The Island Kingdom*, *The Man Who Wrote on Water*, and *The Floating Island*, among other works. His latest work of translation is *The Kingdom of This World* by Alejo Carpentier. He served as president of the Association of Writers and Writing Programs from 2005 to 2006 and has received fellowships from the National Endowment for the Arts, the Rockefeller Foundation, and the Guggenheim Foundation. Currently he lives in Vermont and serves as Distinguished Writer-in-Residence in the Department of Writing, Literature, and Publishing at Emerson College.

W.S. Merwin was born in New York City in 1927 and was United States Poet Laureate in 2010. His first book of poetry, *A Mask for Janus* (1952), was selected by W.H. Auden for the Yale Younger Poets Prize. Merwin has authored dozens of books of poetry and prose and has won many awards, including fellowships from the Rockefeller and the Guggenheim foundations and the National Endowment for the Arts. Merwin's most recent books include *The Essential W.S. Merwin, Garden Time, The Moon before Morning*, and *The Shadow of Sirius*.

María Isabel Lara Millapán is the author of three works of poetry, including *Puliwen ñi Pewma*, and has contributed to anthologies such as *20 poetas mapuche contemporáneos*. She lives in Chile, where she is a professor of language and communication at the Pontificia Universidad Católica de Chile and works to preserve the indigenous Mapuche language and culture.

Moon Tae-jun has published three poetry collections.

Majid Naficy has published more than twenty books of poetry and essays, including *Muddy Shoes* and *Father and Son*. His work has been anthologized in books such as *Poets Against the War* and has been engraved in public places by the city of Los Angeles. He lives in Los Angeles.

Aimee Nezhukumatathil is the author of four books of poetry, most recently *Oceanic*. With Ross Gay, she coauthored the chapbook *Lace & Pyrite: Letters from Two Gardens*. Her honors include a Pushcart Prize and a fellowship from the National Endowment for the Arts. Her collection of nature essays is forthcoming from Milkweed Editions. Nezhukumatathil is a professor of English in the University of Mississippi's MFA program. She lives in Oxford, Mississippi, with her husband, the writer Dustin Parsons, and their two young sons.

Zehra Nigah is an Urdu poet and scriptwriter from Pakistan. She has written several television drama serials and received awards, including Pride of Performance, in recognition of her literary work.

Sharon Olds is the author of *Stag's Leap*, recipient of the Pulitzer Prize and the T.S. Eliot Prize; *The Father*, which was short-listed for the T.S. Eliot Prize and a finalist for the National Book Critics Circle Award; and numerous other works of poetry. Olds held the position of New York State Poet Laureate from 1998 to 2000 and served as a chancellor of the Academy of American Poets from 2006 to 2012. She lives in New Hampshire and New York City, where she is a professor at New York University.

Mary Oliver held the Catharine Osgood Foster Chair for Distinguished Teaching at Bennington College until 2001. In addition to such major awards as the Pulitzer Prize and National Book Award, Oliver received fellowships from the Guggenheim Foundation and the National Endowment for the Arts. She also won the American Academy of Arts and Letters Award and the Poetry Society of America's Shelley Memorial and Alice Fay di Castagnola awards. Her *New and Selected Poems* (1992) won the National Book Award. Oliver passed away in January 2019.

Kira Pelowitz is a student at the New Mexico Institute of Mining and Technology.

Dr. Craig Santos Perez is a native Chamoru (Chamorro) from the Pacific Island of Guåhan (Guam). He is the cofounder of Ala Press, coeditor of three anthologies of Pacific literature, and the author of four collections of poetry. He is an associate professor in the English department at the University of Hawai'i at Manōa, where he teaches creative writing and environmental poetry.

Catherine Pierce is the author of three books of poems: *The Tornado Is the World*, *The Girls of Peculiar*, and *Famous Last Words*, all from Saturnalia Books. Her work has appeared in *Best American Poetry, The American Poetry Review, The Southern Review*, and elsewhere, and has won a Pushcart Prize. She codirects the creative writing program at Mississippi State University.

Carlos Price-Sanchez wrote "Buck Lane" at age eighteen while attending Friend's Central School, Wynnewood, Pennsylvania.

Fabio Pusterla is a Swiss translator and writer in Italian. He has published several collections of poetry, most recently *Corpo Stellare*. He has been awarded the Prix Gottfried Keller, the Premio Letterario Guiseppe Dessì, and the Swiss Schiller prizes. He divides his time between Lombardy, Italy, and Lugano, Switzerland, where he teaches Italian language and literature.

Cecil Rajendra is the author of *Bones and Feathers, Dove on Fire: Poems on Peace, Justice and Ecology*, and *Broken Buds*, among others. He was awarded the first Malaysian Lifetime Humanitarian Award and was nominated for the Nobel Prize. He lives in Penang, Malaysia, where he is a founding member of the Legal Aid Bureau and works as a human-rights lawyer.

Ed Roberson is the author of *Atmosphere Conditions*, which was chosen for the National Poetry Series and was a finalist for the Academy of American Poets' Lenore Marshall Poetry Prize; *To See the Earth Before the End of the World*, which was a runner up for the Los Angeles Times Book Award in Poetry; and *Voices Cast Out to Talk Us In*, which won the Iowa Poetry Prize. He is also the recipient of a PEN/Voelcker Award for Poetry. He lives in Chicago, where he is Distinguished Artist-in-Residence at Northwestern University.

Maya Roe's poem "Midmorning, Summer Rain" was written when the poet was thirteen, in Sonora, California.

Pattiann Rogers is the author of numerous books, including *Quickening Fields, Wayfare*, and *Firekeeper: New and Selected Poems*, which was a finalist for the Lenore Marshall Poetry Prize. In 2018, she was awarded a special John Burroughs Medal for Lifetime Achievement in Nature Poetry. Among other awards, she has received the Tietjens Prize and the Hokin Prize from *Poetry*, a Lannan Fellowship and a Lannan Literary Award, and five Pushcart Prizes. She lives with her husband in Colorado.

Maia Rosenfeld is a three-time national medalist in the Scholastic Art and Writing Awards and a finalist winner in YoungArts. She has also received honors in the Waldman International Art and Writing Competition, the Adroit Prizes, the Ralph Munn Creative Writing Contest, the International Torrance Legacy Creativity Awards, the LVW Student Poetry Contest, and the Norman Mailer Writing Awards. She is an undergraduate at Brown University, where she works as a Bonner Community Fellow at the Swearer Center.

Mary Ruefle is the author of numerous books of poetry, including *My Private Property, A Little White Shadow, The Most of It,* and *The Adamant,* winner of the 1988 Iowa Poetry Prize. She is also the recipient of an Award in Literature from the American Academy of Arts and Letters, a Guggenheim Fellowship, a National Endowment for the Arts

Fellowship, and a Whiting Award. She lives in Bennington, Vermont, where she teaches in the MFA program at Vermont College.

Natasha Sajé is the author of three books of poems: *Red Under the Skin*, *Bend*, and *Vivarium*. She is also the author of *Windows and Doors: A Poet Reads Literary Theory* and a forthcoming book of personal essays, *Terroir: Essays on Otherness*. She is the recipient of Robert Winner and Alice Fay di Castagnola Awards, a Fulbright fellowship, the Campbell Corner Poetry Prize, and the Utah Book Award. Sajé is a professor of English at Westminster College in Salt Lake City and has been teaching in the Vermont College MFA in writing program since 1996.

Silke Scheuermann is a German poet and novelist. Born in Karlsruhe in 1973, she was educated in Frankfurt, Leipzig, and Paris. She is best known for her debut novel *Die Stunde zwischen Hund und Wolf* (*The Hour Between Dog and Wolf*), which has been translated into ten languages, including English. She has won numerous German and European literary prizes and fellowships, including the Georg-Christoph-Lichtenberg-Preis, the Leonce-und-Lena-Preis, the Hölty-Preis, the Bertolt-Brecht-Literaturpreis, and a Villa Massimo fellowship.

Tim Seibles recently finished a two-year appointment as Poet Laureate of Virginia. He is the author of six collections of poetry, including *Fast Animal*, a finalist for the National Book Award; *One Turn Around the Sun*; and *Buffalo Head Solos*. He is the recipient of the PEN Oakland/Josephine Miles Literary Award and the Theodore Roethke Memorial Poetry Prize. A former fellow of the Fine Arts Work Center in Provincetown, Seibles is currently a professor of English at Old Dominion University in Norfolk, Virginia.

Shang Qin is the author of four books of poetry, which have been translated into multiple languages. His work is regularly included in major anthologies of contemporary Chinese literature, most recently in Columbia University's *Frontier Taiwan: An Anthology of Modern Taiwanese Poetry*. He lives in Taiwan.

Betsy Sholl is the author of nine books of poetry, most recently *House of Sparrows: New and Selected Poems*, which received the Four Lakes Prize in Poetry. Other books include *Otherwise Unseeable*, which also received the Four Lakes poetry prize and the Maine Literary Award for Poetry; *Rough Cradle*; and *Late Psalm*. She lives in Portland, Maine, and teaches in the low-residency MFA program at the Vermont College of Fine Arts.

Shu Ting is the pen name of Gōng Pèiyú and the author of works such as *Mist of My Heart: Selected Poems of Shu Ting* and *Selected Poems: An Authorized Collection*. She won the National Outstanding Poetry Award twice and was asked to join the official Chinese Writers' Association.

Lee Slonimsky is the author of *Lion, Gnat, Red-Tailed Hawk on Wall Street*, and *Talk Between Leaf and Skin*. He lives with his wife, Carol Goodman, in New York's Hudson Valley and is the managing partner of Ocean Partners LP and the literary executor of the Daniel Hoffman Literary Estate, which is archived at the Library of Congress.

Tracy K. Smith served as the twenty-second Poet Laureate of the United States from 2017–19. She is the author of four poetry collections, most recently *Wade in the Water* and *Life on Mars*, which was awarded the 2012 Pulitzer Prize. She lives in New Jersey and teaches at Princeton University.

Gary Snyder is the author of *Axe Handles*, which received an American Book Award; *Mountains and Rivers without End*; and *The Practice of the Wild*, among other works. He is the recipient of a Pulitzer Prize, a Bollingen Prize, a John Hay Award for Nature Writing, and a Ruth Lilly Poetry Prize. He was elected a chancellor of the Academy of American Poets in 2003.

Gerald Stern's second poetry collection, *Lucky Life*, was the Lamont Poetry Selection of the Academy of American Poets and was nominated for a National Book Award. Subsequent collections include *Everything Is Burning*; *Save the Last Dance*; and *Early Collected Poems: 1965–1992*, a volume collecting six of Stern's earliest books. Stern taught for many years at the Iowa Writers' Workshop. His many awards and honors include the Wallace Stevens Award, the Bess Hokin Prize, the Ruth Lilly Poetry Prize, the Bernard F. Conners Prize from the *Paris Review*, and the Pennsylvania Governor's Award for Excellence in the Arts.

Talin Tahajian grew up near Boston. Her poetry has appeared in the *Kenyon Review Online*, *Indiana Review*, *Best New Poets* (2014 and 2016), *Black Warrior Review*, and *The Rumpus*. She edits poetry for *Big Lucks* and *The Adroit Journal* and is an MFA candidate at the University of Michigan.

Shuntarō Tanikawa's poetry has been translated into numerous languages, including Chinese, Korean, Mongolian, and many European languages. His collections of poetry in English include *The Selected Poems of Shuntarō Tanikawa* (trans. Harold Wright, 1983); *Floating the River in Melancholy* (trans. William Elliott and Kazuo Kawamura, 1989), which won an American Book Award; *Selected Poems* (trans. William I. Elliott, 2001); and *The Art of Being Alone: Poems 1952–2009* (trans. Takako Lento, 2011). His many honors and awards include a Yomiuri Prize, an Asahi Prize, and a Zhongkun International Poetry Award.

Mark Tredinnick, winner of the Montreal International Poetry Prize, is the author of *Almost Everything I Know, Bluewren Cantos, Fire Diary, The Blue Plateau, The Lyrebird, The Little Red Writing Book,* and seven other works of poetry and prose. His other awards include two Premier's Literary Awards, the Cardiff, Newcastle, ACU, and Blake Poetry Prizes, the Calibre Essay Prize, and the Wildcare Nature Writing Prize. His ecocritical study, *The Land's Wild Music,* is published by Trinity University Press. He teaches at the University of Sydney and University of Technology Sydney. The father of five, he lives and writes along the Wingecarribee River southwest of Sydney, Australia.

Natasha Trethewey served two terms as the nineteenth Poet Laureate of the United States (2012–2014). She is the author of five collections of poetry: *Domestic Work, Bellocq's Ophelia, Native Guard* — for which she was awarded the 2007 Pulitzer Prize — *Thrall,* and, most recently, *Monument.* In 2010 she published a book of nonfiction, *Beyond Katrina: A Meditation on the Mississippi Gulf Coast.* She is the recipient of fellowships from the Academy of American Poets, the National Endowment for the Arts, the

Guggenheim Foundation, the Rockefeller Foundation, the Beinecke Library at Yale, and the Radcliffe Institute for Advanced Study at Harvard. In 2013 she was inducted into the American Academy of Arts and Sciences, and in 2017 she received the Heinz Award for Arts and Humanities.

Kirmen Uribe is the author of multiple novels and poetry collections, including *Elkarrekin esnatzeko ordua*, winner of a Spanish Critics Award; *Bilbao-New York-Bilbao*, winner of a Spanish Critics Award and Spanish National Book Award; and *Bitartean heldu eskutik*, which has also received a Spanish Critics Award and was translated into Spanish, French, English, Catalan, and Russian. He grew up near Bilbao in the Basque region.

Jean Valentine is the author of more than a dozen collections of poetry, including *The River at Wolf*; *Little Boat*; *Door in the Mountain: New and Collected Poems, 1965–2003*, which won the National Book Award; *Break the Glass*, a finalist for the Pulitzer Prize; and *Shirt in Heaven*. She has been awarded a Bunting Institute Fellowship, a Guggenheim Foundation Fellowship, the Shelley Memorial Award, the Wallace Stevens Award, and the 2017 Bollingen Prize for Poetry.

Selene Jazmín Venegas was a finalist in the 2015 River of Words Poetry Contest. Venegas lives in Amatlán de Quetzalcóatl, México.

Wendy Videlock is the author of the chapbook *What's That Supposed to Mean* and the full-length collections *Slingshots & Love Plums*, *The Dark Gnu and Other Poems*, and *Nevertheless*. A regular contributor to *Poetry,* Wendy lives on the western slope of the Colorado Rockies, where she writes, paints, and teaches.

Anne Waldman is the author of *The Iovis Trilogy: Colors in the Mechanism of Concealment*, which won the PEN Center USA Award; *Marriage: A Sentence*; and *Fast Speaking Woman: Chants and Essays*, among others. She has received the American Book Award for Lifetime Achievement and the Dylan Thomas Memorial Award, as well as many others. She divides her time between Greenwich Village in New York City and Boulder, Colorado, where she is the director of the MFA creative writing and poetics program at Naropa University.

Jessica Walker is a poet living and working in New York. She has received the Foyle Young Poets of the Year Award and the Cumbria Young Writers Award, and her poetry has been published by The Poetry Society; Tower Poetry, in their anthology *Something to Be Said*; and *Cadaverine Magazine.* Her work has also appeared in various publications by York St John University, most notably as a featured poem in their student showcase and the *Beyond the Walls* anthology.

Charles Wright was the fiftieth Poet Laureate of the United States. He is the author of numerous collections of poems, including *Country Music: Selected Early Poems*, cowinner of the 1983 National Book Award for Poetry, and *Black Zodiac*, winner of a National Book Critics Circle Award and a Pulitzer Prize. He has also received a Ruth Lilly Poetry Prize.

Patricia Young is the author of twelve poetry collections—most recently, *Amateurs at Love*—and one book of short fiction. Her poems have been widely anthologized and have also appeared in six chapbooks and numerous magazines and journals. She has twice been nominated for the Governor General's Literary Award for poetry and has won the Pat Lowther Memorial Award, the Dorothy Livesay Poetry Prize, the CBC Poetry Prize, the Bliss Carman Poetry Award, the Confederation Poets Prize, and several National Magazine Awards. She lives in Victoria, British Columbia.

Adam Zagajewski is the author of many collections of poetry, including *Anteny, Powrót,* and *Pragnienie.* He has been awarded the Neustadt International Prize for Literature, the Griffin Poetry Prize Lifetime Recognition Award, and the Princess of Asturias Award for Literature. He splits his time between Paris, France, where he is coeditor of *Zeszyty literackie,* and Houston, Texas, where he serves as visiting associate professor of English in the creative writing program at the University of Houston.

Translators

Zaia Alexander's works include *Wende Kids: A New Generation of German Authors* and a translation of Antje Rávic Strubel's novel *Snowed Under,* among other works. She has served as chair of the PEN Center Translation Jury and director of programs at the Villa Aurora in Pacific Palisades and received a Lannan Literary residency. She lives in Los Angeles and Berlin.

Agnar Artúvertin is a writer, poet, publisher, and translator with seventeen books to date. A member of three Scandinavian writers' associations, he has translated tales from *The Arabian Nights* and works by Sappho, Blake, Pushkin, Poe, and Kafka. He lives in the Faroe Islands.

Darcy Lee Brandel has published work on Gertrude Stein, Grace Paley, and other experimental women writers and, along with Chae-Pyong Song, translations of Korean Buddhist poetry. She taught as a professor of English and chair of the Department of English and Modern Languages at Marygrove College for twelve years, where she also served as director of the English graduate program, secretary of the Faculty Assembly, and established the first Women's Center at the college. She currently teaches in the Residential College at the University of Michigan as part of the Semester in Detroit program.

Steve Brock is the author of *The Night Is a Dying Dog* and *Double Glaze* and the cotranslator, along with Sergio Holas, Víctor Cifuentes Palacios, and Juan Garrido Salgado, of *Poetry of the Earth: Mapuche Trilingual Anthology.* He lives with his wife and daughter in Adelaide, Australia.

Clare Cavanagh is the author of works such as *Lyric Poetry and Modern Politics: Russia, Poland, and the West,* which received a National Book Critics Circle Award for Criticism, and *Osip Mandelstam and the Modernist Creation of Tradition.* She has also received a William Riley Parker Prize from the Modern Language Association and the American Association of Teachers of Slavic and East European Languages Prize for Outstanding Scholarly Book on Slavic Literature, among other awards. She is the Frances Hooper Professor in the Arts and Humanities, Slavic Languages and Literatures, and Comparative Literary Studies departments at Northwestern University.

Chad Davidson is the author of *From the Fire Hills, The Last Predicta,* and *Consolation Miracle,* among other works. His poems and articles have appeared in *AGNI, Colorado*

Review, Hotel Amerika, The Paris Review, and elsewhere. He lives in Carrollton, Georgia, where he is an associate professor of English at the University of West Georgia.

Sasha Dugdale is the author of four poetry collections, including *Joy*, which won a Forward Prize for Best Single Poem and The Poetry Book Society Winter Choice Award; *Red House*; and *The Estate*. She is also a playwright and translator of Russian poetry and drama. She lives in southeast England, where she codirects the Winchester Poetry Festival.

Marella Feltrin is a scholar and translator of Italian literature. Her translation of Paola Masino's 1945 novel, *Birth and Death of the Housewife,* was published by SUNY Press in 2009. She is an associate professor in the Department of Modern Languages and Literatures at Ithaca College.

Donald Finkel was the author of *A Joyful Noise, The Garbage Wars*, and *Answer Back*. He taught at the Iowa Writers' Workshop, Bard College, and Washington University in St. Louis. Born in the Bronx, New York City, he died in St. Louis in 2008.

Forrest Gander is the author of *Be With*; *Core Samples from the World*, which was a finalist for the Pulitzer Prize and the National Book Critics Circle Award; *Redstart: An Ecological Process*; and *Science & Steepleflower*.

Sam Hamill was a founder of Copper Canyon Press. His works include *Destination Zero: Poems 1970-1995, Measured by Stone, Habitation: Collected Poems,* and *Almost Paradise: New and Selected Poems and Translations.* He was awarded fellowships from the National Endowment for the Arts, the Guggenheim Foundation, the Woodrow Wilson Foundation, and the Mellon Fund, and won the Stanley Lindberg Lifetime Achievement Award for Editing and the Washington Poets Association Lifetime Achievement Award. He passed away on April 14, 2018.

Sergio Holas is the author of *Distancia cero, Ciudad dividida,* and *Paisajes en movimiento* and the cotranslator, along with Juan Garrido Salgado, Víctor Cifuentes Palacios, and Steve Brock, of the trilingual *Poetry of the Earth: Mapuche Trilingual Anthology.* He lives in Adelaide, Australia, where he teaches Spanish language and Latin American culture and literature at the University of Adelaide.

Xuefei Jin (Ha Jin) is the author of *Waiting,* which received a National Book Award and a PEN/Faulkner award; *War Trash, The Crazed,* and *The Bridegroom,* among numerous other works. He has also received a PEN/Hemingway award for his first collection of short stories, *Ocean of Words,* and the Flannery O'Connor Award for Short Fiction for his second, *Under the Red Flag.* He lives in Boston, Massachusetts, where he is a professor of English at Boston University.

Tsipi Keller's most recent translation is *You Who Cross My Path* by Erez Bilton. She is the recipient of several literary awards, including a National Endowment for the Arts Translation Fellowship, a New York Foundation for the Arts grant, and an Armand G. Erpf award from Columbia University.

Waqas Khwaja is the author of four works of poetry, including *Hold Your Breath* and *No One Waits for the Train,* and the editor of three anthologies of Pakistani literature:

Cactus, Mornings in the Wilderness, and *Pakistani Short Stories.* He has received special recognition for outstanding creative writing from the South Asian Literary Association and served as translation editor for *Modern Poetry of Pakistan,* a National Endowment of the Arts project. He is Ellen Douglass Leyburn Professor of English at Agnes Scott College in Decatur, Georgia.

Carolyn Kizer was the author of *Pro femina; Mermaids in the Basement: Poems for Women; Cool, Calm, and Collected: Poems;* and *Yin,* among other works. Her awards included the Frost Medal, the Theodore Roethke Memorial Poetry Award, and an American Academy of Arts and Letters Award. She served as a chancellor of the Academy of American Poets. Kizer passed away on October 9, 2014.

Skye Lavin is a graduate of the Iowa Writer's Workshop and is currently based in Madison, Wisconsin.

Denise Levertov was the author of more than twenty collections of poetry and prose, including *Tesserae: Memories and Suppositions, Evening Train,* and *A Door in the Hive.* She received the Shelley Memorial Award, the Robert Frost Medal, the Lenore Marshall Poetry Prize, the Lannan Award, and grants and fellowships from the National Institute of Arts and Letters and Guggenheim Foundation. She was born in Essex, England, and died in Seattle, Washington.

Alexis Levitin has published more than forty books of translation, including Clarice Lispector's *Soulstorm,* Eugénio de Andrade's *Forbidden Words,* and Salgado Maranhão's *Blood of the Sun.* He was also the editor of *Brazil: A Traveler's Literary Companion.* He is the recipient of National Endowment for the Arts Translation Fellowships, two Fulbright Senior Lecturer Awards, and a Witter Bynner Foundation for Poetry Translation Grant, among other awards. He is a professor of English at the State University of New York, Plattsburgh.

Elizabeth Macklin is the author of *You've Just Been Told* and *A Woman Kneeling in the Big City.* She has received a Guggenheim Fellowship and an Ingram Merrill poetry prize. She splits her time between New York City and Bilbao in the Basque region, where she works as a translator for the Basque Literature Series.

John H. McGlynn is an editor and translator who is best known for his works *Illuminations: The Writing Traditions of Indonesia, The Mute's Soliloquy,* and *Indonesia in the Soeharto Years.* He is the Indonesian country editor for Manōa, a founding member of the Asia Pacific Writers & Translators Association, and a trustee of the American Indonesian Exchange Foundation, which oversees the Fulbright and Humphrey scholarship programs in Indonesia. He lives in Jakarta, Indonesia.

Catherine Rodriguez-Nieto has translated numerous works of literature from Spanish to English, including *Fireflight: Three Latin American Poets* and *Palabras de mediodía/ Noon Words.*

Juan Garrido Salgado has published three books of poetry and has translated works such as MTC Cronin's *Talking to Neruda's Questions.* He has also worked with Aboriginal poets to create *Espejo de Tierra/Earth Mirror Poetry Anthology* and with Steve Brock, Víctor Cifuentes Palacios, and Sergio Holas to translate *Poetry of the Earth: Mapuche Trilingual Anthology*. He lives in Adelaide, Australia.

Mark Schafer has translated works by Latin American authors Alberto Ruy Sánchez, Virgilio Piñera, Jesús Gardea, Antonio José Ponte, Sonia Rivera-Valdés, Gloria Gervitz, and others. He has received the Robert Fitzgerald Prize, two translation fellowships from the National Endowment for the Arts, a grant from the Fund for Culture Mexico/USA, and a residency at the Banff International Literary Translation Centre, among other awards. He is a lecturer in Spanish and translation and co-coordinator of the Spanish-English Translation Certificate Program in the Hispanic Studies Department at the University of Massachusetts at Boston.

Lawrence Schimel has published over one hunded titles as author or anthologist, including the poetry collection *Desayuno en la cama,* the graphic novel *Vacaciones en Ibiza,* the novel *Una barba para dos,* and children's books such as *Igual que ellos,* which was selected by the International Board on Books for Young People as an Outstanding Book for Young People with Disabilities. He is a founding member of the Publishing Triangle, an organization of lesbian and gay writers in the publishing industry, which he has chaired for two terms.

Saadi A. Simawe was an author, teacher, and translator, most known for his works *Black Orpheus: Music in African American Fiction from the Harlem Renaissance to Toni Morrison* and *Iraqi Poetry Today,* for which he was an editor. He taught for over twenty years as an associate professor of English at Grinnell College. He passed away on February 19, 2017.

Dr. Chae-Pyong Song was a poet, scholar, and translator. His publications include works on postcolonial literature and theory and translations that have appeared in the *Korea Times, New Writing from Korea, Metamorphoses: Journal of Literary Translation, WSQ: Women's Studies Quarterly, Illuminations,* and *Azalea: Journal of Korean Literature and Culture.* He received numerous awards, including the fortieth Korean Literature Translation Award for his translation of Kim Hyesoon's poems. He passed away on February 12, 2013.

Martin Sorrell's publications in the field of translation include *Rimbaud: Collected Poems, Verlaine: Selected Poems, Elles: A Bilingual Anthology of Modern French Poetry by Women,* and three plays by Molière. He has written original plays and stories for BBC radio and has won two major translation prizes. He is a professor of literary translation at the University of Exeter in South West England.

A.E. Stallings was a 2011 MacArthur Fellow. She is the author of *Olives,* which was a finalist for the National Book Critics Circle Award; *Hapax,* which was awarded the Poets' Prize; and *Archaic Smile.* She lives in Athens, Greece, where she is the director of the poetry program at the Athens Centre.

Frank Stewart is an essayist, translator, and author of four books of poetry, including *By All Means* and *Flying the Red Eye.* He also edited the anthology *The Poem Behind* *the Poem: Translating Asian Poetry*. He has received a Whiting Award and the Hawai'i Governor's Award for Literature. He teaches in the Department of English at the University of Hawai'i at Manōa.

Niloufar Talebi is a writer, translator, and theater artist. She is the author of numerous works, including *Belonging: New Poetry by Iranians Around the World*, *Atash Sorushan* (Fire Angels), and *The Persian Rite of Spring*. She is the recipient of a Literature Translation Fellowship from the National Endowment of the Arts, a PEN/New York State Council on the Arts grant, and the International Center for Writing and Translation Prize, among other awards. She lives in the San Francisco Bay Area.

Harold Wright is a poet, scholar, and translator of numerous works of Japanese poetry. He is a recipient of a grant for translation from the National Endowment for the Arts and taught for seven years at Antioch College as a professor of Japanese language and literature. He lives in Yellow Springs, Ohio, with his wife.

Michelle Yeh is an author, editor, and translator whose works include *Modern Chinese Poetry: Theory and Practice Since 1917*, *Anthology of Modern Chinese Poetry*, *No Trace of the Gardener: Poems of Yang Mu*, and *Frontier Taiwan: An Anthology of Modern Chinese Poetry*. She is Distinguished Professor of Chinese at University of California, Davis.

Contributors' Acknowledgments

The editor and publisher gratefully acknowledge the permissions granted to reproduce the copyrighted material in this book. Every effort has been made to trace copyright holders and to obtain their permission for the use of copyrighted material. The publisher apologizes for any errors or omissions in the following list and would be grateful to be notified of any corrections that should be incorporated in future reprints or editions of this book.

Chris Abani, "Descent" from *Sanctificum*. Copyright © 2013 by Chris Abani. Reprinted with the permission of Copper Canyon Press.

Julia Alvarez, "Bilingual Sestina" from *The Other Side/El otro lado*. Copyright © 1995 by Julia Alvarez. Published by Plume/Penguin, a division of Penguin Group (USA). Originally published in *The George Washington Review*. By permission of Susan Bergholz Literary Services, New York, NY, and Lamy, NM. All rights reserved.

Francisco Aragón, "Far Away" from *The Wind Shifts: New Latino Poetry*, edited by Francisco Aragón. Copyright © 2007, The Arizona Board of Regents. Reprinted with the permission of the University of Arizona Press.

Betye Arrastia-Nowak, "I Am Like a Caterpillar" (2014) from the 7th Grade Poetry Foundation. Reprinted with the permission of the author.

James Arthur, "Wind" from Poem-a-Day (Academy of American Poets, September 21, 2017). Copyright © 2017 by James Arthur. Reprinted with the permission of the author.

Fadhil Assultani, "A Tree" from *Iraqi Poetry Today*, edited by Saadi A. Simawe. Copyright © 2002. Reprinted with permission.

Ela Aster, "On the Street of Nature" from *A Neighborhood of Poems* (Poets House, 2013). Copyright © by Ela Aster. Reprinted with permission.

Margaret Atwood, "Elegy for the Giant Tortoises" from *Selected Poems 1965–1975*. Copyright © 1976 by Margaret Atwood. Reprinted by permission of Houghton Mifflin Harcourt Publishing Company. All rights reserved.

Gabeba Baderoon, "My Tongue Softens on the Other Name" from *The Dream in the Next Body*. Copyright © 2005 by Gabeba Baderoon. Reprinted with the permission of Kwela Books.

David Baker, "Bright Pitch" from *Never-Ending Birds*. Copyright © 2011 by David Baker. Used by permission of W.W. Norton & Company, Inc.

Griffon Bannon, "How to Be a Hawk" from *River of Words: Winners of the River of Words 20th Annual Environmental Poetry & Art Contest*. Copyright © 2015 River of Words. Reprinted with the permission of River of Words Press.

Jesús J. Barquet, "Robinson" from *Island of My Hunger*. Copyright © 2007 by Jesús J.

Ross Gay, "Poem for My Child, If Ever You Shall Be" from *Bringing the Shovel Down*. Copyright © 2011 by Ross Gay. Reprinted by permission of the University of Pittsburgh Press.

Mordechai Geldman, "Almost Flowers" from *Poets on the Edge: An Anthology of Contemporary Hebrew Poetry* (Albany, NY: SUNY Press, 2008), translated by Tsipi Keller. Reprinted with the permission of SUNY Press.

Danielle Legros Georges, "Intersection" from *The Dear Remote Nearness of You*. Copyright © 2016 by Danielle Legros Georges. Reprinted with the permission of the author and Barrow Street Press.

Nikki Giovanni, "Walking Down Park" from *The Collected Poetry of Nikki Giovanni, 1968–1998*. Copyright © 2003 by Nikki Giovanni. Reprinted by permission of HarperCollins Publishers.

Rigoberto González, "The Slaughterhouse" from *So Often the Pitcher Goes to Water until It Breaks*. Copyright © 1999 by Rigoberto González. Used with the permission of the University of Illinois Press.

Lorna Goodison, "Lepidopterist" from *Selected Poems*. Copyright © 1999 by Lorna Goodison. Reprinted with the permission of the University of Michigan Press.

Joy Goswami, "The Burning Bird Drops," reprinted with the permission of the author and translator.

Rachel Eliza Griffiths, "The Human Zoo" from *Lighting the Shadow*. Copyright © 2015 by Rachel Eliza Griffiths. Reprinted with the permission of The Permissions Company, Inc., on behalf of Four Way Books.

Jennifer Grotz, "Poppies" from *Window Left Open*. Copyright © 2016 by Jennifer Grotz. Reprinted with the permission of The Permissions Company, Inc., on behalf of Graywolf Press.

Paul Guest, "Post-Factual Love Poem" from Poem-a-Day (American Academy of Poets, July 17, 2017). Reprinted with permission.

Noa Gur-Arie, "Dolbear's Law" from *The Best Teen Writing of 2014*. Copyright © 2014. Reprinted with the permission of Scholastic, Inc.

Hadley, "The Mighty Guardian" from *Poetry on Our Terms: Winners of the 2016 7th Grade Poetry Contest*. Copyright © 2016 by 7th Grade Poetry Foundation. Reprinted with permission.

Kimiko Hahn, "The Fever" from *Toxic Flora*. Copyright © 2010 by Kimiko Hahn. Used by permission of W.W. Norton & Company, Inc.

Kendra Hamilton, "Southern Living" from *The Goddess of Gumbo: Poems* (Word Press, 2006). Reprinted with the permission of the author.

Joy Harjo, "The Path to the Milky Way" from *A Map to the Next World*. Copyright © 2010 by Joy Harjo. Used by permission of W.W. Norton & Company, Inc.

David Hart, "Naming the Field" from *Field Days*. Copyright © 1988 by David Hart. Reprinted with the permission of Green Books.

Robert Hass, "Meditation at Lagunitas" from *Praise*. Copyright © 1999 by Robert Hass. Reprinted by permission of HarperCollins Publishers.

Louise Herlin, "The gull inch-perfect over water" from *Modern French Poetry*, selected and translated by Martin Sorrell (Forest Books, 1992). Copyright © 1992 by Martin Sorrell. Reprinted with the permission of the author.

Lee Herrick, "A Thousand Saxophones" from *Hurricane Blues* (Southeast Missouri State University Press, 2006). Copyright © 2006 by Lee Herrick. Reprinted with the permission of the author.

Bob Hicok, "Hold your breath: a song of climate change" from *Hold*. Copyright © 2018 by Bob Hicok. Reprinted with the permission of Copper Canyon Press.

Brenda Hillman, "The Seeds Talk Back to Monsanto" from *Seasonal Works with Letters on Fire*. Copyright © 2016 by Brenda Hillman. Published by Wesleyan University Press. Used by permission.

Krassin Himmirsky, "The Cricket," translated by Denise Levertov from *The Hudson Review* (Winter 1983). Translation copyright © 1983 by Denise Levertov. Reprinted with the permission of the Denise Levertov Literary Trust.

Jane Hirshfield, "The Weighing" from *The October Palace*. Copyright © 1994 by Jane Hirshfield. Reprinted by permission of HarperCollins Publishers.

Huang Canran, "Come Back to the Mountain," translated by Ha Jin, from *Another Kind of Nation: An Anthology of Contemporary Chinese Poetry*, edited by Zhang Er and Chen D. Dongdong (Talisman House, 2007). Reprinted with the permission of the author and translator.

David Huerta, "Before the Protest in the Streets Is Dispersed" from *Before Saying Any of the Great Words*. Copyright © 2009 by David Huerta. Reprinted with the permission of Copper Canyon Press.

Katerina Iliopoulou, "The Fox" from *The Book of the Soil*, translated by A.E. Stallings (Melani, 2016). Translation copyright © 2016 by A.E. Stallings. Reprinted with the permission of the poet and the translator.

Richard Jackson, "The Voices" from *Retrievals*. Reprinted with the permission of C&R Press.

Joan Naviyuk Kane, "The Straits" from *Milk Black Carbon*. Copyright © 2017 by Joan Naviyuk Kane. Reprinted by permission of University of Pittsburgh Press.

Jaan Kaplinski, "From childhood on" from *The Wandering Border*, translated by the author with Sam Hamill and Riina Tamm. Copyright © 1987 by Jaan Kaplinski. Reprinted with the permission of Copper Canyon Press.

Laura Kasischke, "Pregnant at the All-Night Supermarket" from *Fire and Flower*. Copyright © 1998 by Laura Kasischke. Reprinted with the permission of The Permissions Company, Inc., on behalf of Alice James Books.

and Sergio Holas. Reprinted with permission of Interactive Publications Pty Ltd., Brisbane Australia.

Moon Tae-jun, "The Ibis," translated by Chae-Pyong Song and Darcy Brandel. Reprinted with the permission of Darcy Brandel, PhD.

Majid Naficy, "To a Snail" from *Belonging: New Poetry by Iranians Around the World*, edited and translated by Niloufar Talebi, published by North Atlantic Books. Copyright © 2008 by Niloufar Talebi. Reprinted by permission of the publisher.

Aimee Nezhukumatathil, "Invitation" from *Oceanic*. Copyright © 2018 by Aimee Nezhukumatathil. Reprinted with the permission of Copper Canyon Press.

Zehra Nigah, "Evening's First Star," translated by Waqas Khwaja, from *Modern Poetry of Pakistan*. Copyright © 2010 by Waqas Khwaja. Reprinted with the permission of Dalkey Archive Press.

Sharon Olds, "Ode to the Last Thirty-Eight Trees in New York City Visible from This Window" from *Odes*. Copyright © 2016 by Sharon Olds. Used by permission of Alfred A. Knopf, an imprint of the Knopf Doubleday Publishing Group, a division of Penguin Random House LLC. All rights reserved.

Mary Oliver, "The Fish" from *American Primitive*. Copyright © 1983 by Mary Oliver. Reprinted with the permission of Little, Brown and Company. All rights reserved.

Kira Pelowitz, "In the Summer" from *The Best Teen Writing of 2013*. Copyright © 2013. Reprinted with the permission of Scholastic, Inc.

Craig Santos Perez, from "understory: for my pregnant wife, nālani, during her second trimester" from *from unincorporated territory [lukao]* (Omnidawn, 2017). Originally in *Poetry* (January 2016). Reprinted with permission.

Catherine Pierce, "Planet" from *Southern Review* (Spring 2017). Copyright © 2017 by Catherine Pierce. Reprinted with the permission of the author.

Carlos Price-Sanchez, "Buck Lane" from *2014 National Catalog*. Copyright © 2014. Reprinted with the permission of Scholastic, Inc.

Fabio Pusterla, "Star, Meteor, Some Shooting Thing," translated by Chad Davidson and Marella Feltrin, from *Italian Poetry Review* 3 (2008). Reprinted with the permission of the translators.

Cecil Rajendra, "My Message" from *Hour of Assasins and Other Poems* (Bogle-L'Ouverture, 1983). Reprinted with the permission of the author.

Ed Roberson, "sonnet" ("be careful") from *When Thy King Is a Boy*. Copyright © 1970 by Ed Roberson. Reprinted by permission of the University of Pittsburgh Press.

Maya Roe, "Midmorning, Summer Rain." Copyright © 2015 by River of Words. Reprinted with the permission of River of Words Press.

Pattiann Rogers, "A Very Common Field" from *Song of the World Becoming*. Copyright © 2001 by Pattiann Rogers. Reprinted with the permission of Milkweed Editions.

Maia Rosenfeld, "Snapchat Summer" from *The Best Teen Writing 2015*. Copyright © 2015. Reprinted with the permission of Scholastic, Inc.

The book you are holding is a testament to the diverse community of passionate readers who supported *Here: Poems for the Planet*. Copper Canyon Press is deeply grateful to the following individuals around the world whose philanthropic vision and love of poetry made this anthology possible. We have published *Here: Poems for the Planet* together.

Thank you!

Activate World
Lynne and
    Shawn Aebi
Virginia Agnew
Samuel Alexander
Virginia Anderson
Janet Eulalia
    Anderson
Richard Andrews
    and Colleen
    Chartier
Janeen Armstrong
Margaret Armstrong
Carol Bawden and
    Scott Craig
Jeffery Beam and
    Stanley Finch
Joseph Bednarik
Frances Beinecke
Carole P. Beller
Liza and
    William Bennett
Kitty Bergel
Dana Bettinger
Greg Bishop
Melissa, Michael,
    Joshua, and
    Caleb Black
Ron Bloodworth
Michael A. Boyd
Kathleen Brannigan
Traci Brimhall
Louise Brown
Laura Buccieri
Jane and
    Vincent Buck
Dori Cahn and
    Jay W. Stansell

Ralph Calder
Alfred E.
    Cambridge, Jr.
J. Morgan Carney
Frank Carsey
John Claxton
Merilee Clunis
    and Margaret
    Schonfield
Bonnie Colby
Emily E. Conn
Rio Cortez
Robbie R. Cox
Craig Cramer
Constance
    Crawford
Averill Curdy and
    Lynn Geri
Josephine Grace
    Curry
Sofie Jane Dahl
Cheryl S.
    Dannenbring
Robert Dealy
Cecile and J.D.
    Delafield
Michelle Demers
Susan DeWitt
    Davie
Kathleen Dickeman
Gary Dobson
In memory of
    Carl Douglas
Beth and
    Terry Drayton
Catherine Edwards
Margaret Eissler
Dr. Jane Ellingwood

Elaina Ellis
Jane Ellis and
    Jack Litewka
Nancy Marie Faaren
FCB/Clark Street
    Bridge
Beroz Ferrell
Alexandra Fidyk
Laura B. Fjeld
Rebecca Joy
    Fletcher
Julie Fowler
Jonah Lee Fox
Hathaway Barry
    in honor of
    Mira Yli FoxBarry
Jerry Fulks
Aileen Gagney
Helette Gagnon
Carl Galeana
Majda Talal Gama
Loretta Gase
Paula and John
    Gavin
James Allen Giles
Glass Heart String
    Choir
Sierra Golden
Jeffrey Gordinier
Therese "Tag"
    Goulet
Lewis Williams Gray
Deborah Green
Kip and Stanley
    Greenthal
Emily Grise
Karen A. Grooms,
    née Napen

David and
    Joan Grubin
Krzysztof Gruszka
    and Rauni
Sophia Gutherz
Doug and
    Charlotte Guyman
Martha Habecker
Pamela Haferman
Marilyn Halonen
Eleanor and
    Gary Hamilton
Adina Hoffman and
    Peter Cole
Elizabeth Hoile
Donald Holzer
Warren V Hunt
Katherine Ann
    Janeway
Alex Johnson
Pam and Jack Jolley
Robert Jolly
Sarah E. Jones
James Jordan
Mimi Lepreau Jose
Victoria Kaplan
Olivia Katherine
    and Celine
    Lucienne
Patrick Gage Kelley
Margaret Kirk
In honor of George
    Knotek
Aleksey Kovalyov
Robert Larson
Dr. Rebecca Jill
    Leaver
Dana Levin

Don and
  Carla Lewis
Ali Tucker
  Lichtenstein
Michael Lieberman
Joyce Loubere
Maggie Cheney
  Macdonald
Monica Macguire
  and Peter Badame
Sallie Rose Madrone
Suman Mallick,
  Bella Mallick
Emily L. Mankowski
Natalie Martínez
Adelaide Honour
  Mason
Kara and
  Ken Masters
Larry Mawby
In memory
  of Brendan
  McManus
Ronni Meltzer
Mary Ellen Miller
Roger Mitchell
Gwendolyn Morgan
Diana Morley
Elizabeth Mornin
Joseph P. Morra
Leslie J. Muir
Robin Mullet
Joan Murphy
Heather Newbold
Julie and
  Erik Nordstrom

Jan North
Sage Mushin Okura
Sharon L. Oriel
Mary Pat and
  John Osterhaus
Robin Ostow
Sherry Owens
Kisha Palmer
Dan Paquette
H. Stewart Parker
Pascal and
  Jasper Parsons
Walter Parsons
John Pierce
Kimberley
  Pittman-Schulz
Tonya Plank
POEM: People Of
  Earth Matter
Scott Pomfret
John Pound
Brendan Quinn
Carey Radebaugh
Sophie and
  Ella Raymond
Ellen Reardon
Bruce Redwine
Ohana Resnick
James Richardson
Joel and
  Ginger Richman
In memory of
  Sandra E. Riordan
Alberto Ríos
Jeanmarie Riquelme
Sara Ritter

In honor of Simon,
  Beatrice, and
  Graham Ritter
  and Benjamin
  Blumenthal
Joseph C. Roberts
Linda M. Robertson
Karen Rogers
Alida Rol
Lee and Stuart Rolfe
F. Peter Rose
John P. Rosenberg
David Schifeling
Sherry and
  Greg Schuler
Mainon A.
  Schwartz
Nick Scott
Nina Segre
Heidi Sewall
Natalie Shapero
Michael Smallwood
Randall Steven
  Smith
Bernard Smith
Mary Kay
  Sneeringer and
  David Brewster
Stacy L. Spencer
  and Thomas N.
  Ciantra
Douglass
  St. Christian
Delphine and
  Charles Stevens
Randy Sturgis

Kim and
  George Suyama
Thomas Thomas
Mark Tredinnick
Cato Vandrare
Joan and Kurt
  Griffiths Vega
Rachael Amy
  Vickerman
Brandon Michael
  Ward
In memory of
  Charles Weiss
Madeline J. White
Mary Lou and
  Jim Wickwire
Michael Wiegers
Lance Wilcox
Sara Winkelman
In honor of Nancy
  Baker Wise
Marcia Johnson
  Witter
Trina Woldt
Sara and
  Ted Woolsey
Jenny Wyatt

Poetry is vital to language and living. Since 1972, Copper Canyon Press has published extraordinary poetry from around the world to engage the imaginations and intellects of readers, writers, booksellers, librarians, teachers, students, and donors.

WE ARE GRATEFUL FOR THE MAJOR SUPPORT PROVIDED BY:

THE PAUL G. ALLEN
FAMILY FOUNDATION

golden lasso

Anonymous (3)
Jill Baker and Jeffrey Bishop
Anne and Geoffrey Barker
Donna and Matt Bellew
John Branch
Diana Broze
The Beatrice R. and Joseph A. Coleman Foundation, Inc.
Laurie and Oskar Eustis
Mimi Gardner Gates
Nancy Gifford
Gull Industries, Inc. on behalf of William True
The Trust of Warren A. Gummow
Petunia Charitable Fund and advisor Elizabeth Hebert
Bruce Kahn
Phil Kovacevich and Eric Wechsler
Lakeside Industries, Inc.
on behalf of Jeanne Marie Lee
Maureen Lee and Mark Busto

TO LEARN MORE ABOUT UNDERWRITING
COPPER CANYON PRESS TITLES,
PLEASE CALL 360-385-4925 EXT. 103

WE ARE GRATEFUL FOR THE MAJOR SUPPORT PROVIDED BY:

Rhoady Lee and Alan Gartenhaus

Peter Lewis

Ellie Mathews and Carl Youngmann as The North Press

Hank Meijer

Gregg Orr

Gay Phinny

Suzie Rapp and Mark Hamilton

Emily and Dan Raymond

Jill and Bill Ruckelshaus

Kim and Jeff Seely

Richard Swank

Dan Waggoner

Barbara and Charles Wright

Caleb Young as C. Young Creative

The dedicated interns and faithful volunteers
of Copper Canyon Press

The Chinese character for poetry is made up of two parts: "word" and "temple." It also serves as pressmark for Copper Canyon Press.

The text is set in Farnham, designed by Christian Schwartz. The headings are set in Sanuk Big and Sanuk Rounded, designed by Xavier Dupré. Book design by VJBScribe. Printed on archival-quality paper.